EMOTIONAL PRISONER
TRAPPED
BEHIND THE BARS OF
MY
THOUGHTS

José Villegas III

(Re-edited 2005)

Copyright © 2002

Inquiries should be addressed to:
José Villegas III
P.O. Box 10092
Washington, DC 20018
www.JVwinner.com
Phone: 800-958-6337

Cover design: Erick DeVonne Gilbert, Georgia
Editor: Angela Bernardette Tilghman-Taylor, Maryland

ISBN 0-9725067-0-5

DEDICATION

I dedicate this book to my wife, daughters, my family, and friends who made it possible by sticking by me when times were hard and I was struggling. Thanks a million.

ACKNOWLEDGMENTS

First and foremost, I want to give thanks to the indwelling Spirit of God for giving me the insight and courage to write such an honest book.

Second, I want to give thanks to the world for allowing me to grow in spite of myself.

EMOTIONS
ARE THE WARDEN
THAT RUNS THE

PRISON OF OUR
MINDS

WHERE THE SPIRIT
IS SERVING
TIME

TABLE OF CONTENTS

INTRODUCTION

AN <u>EMOTIONAL PRISONER: TRAPPED BEHIND THE BARS OF MY THOUGHTS</u> is a word picture of how I lived my life. Picture being trapped in your mind by your emotions and the only way to be free is by using the key of honesty. We live in a time where emotions are running our lives out of control. Because we seek pleasure to avoid pain, but to avoid pain keeps us in pain. What pain? The pain of our childhood's that are the emotions that create the bars of our thoughts that keep us trapped in the prison of our minds. *Pain is necessary but suffering is optional.* We suffer because we don't learn from the pain, so it keeps repeating itself until we change or die. Pain is a gift that nobody wants. If it weren't for pain, how would we know what to change? A life run by emotions is like being on a roller coaster ride – up and down, round and round.

As children, we were put on the ride without our permission and, as adults we don't know how to get off so we just hold on and holler. It usually takes a lot of pain and suffering before we take a hard, honest look at our lives and muster up the courage to do something about it and change. There is a saying that says, *"Time heals all wounds"* but that's not necessarily so. There are wounds that get worse with time. They are mental and emotional wounds that can only be healed through exposure to the light of truth. Mental and emotional pain never dies but is buried alive and will continue to destroy our lives.

The focus of this book is to share my mental and emotional bondage and, through lots of work on my mind, my freedom. I hope this book will help you do the same. You see, the only difference between you and I is our address because we basically go through the same things and feel the same way. The problem is that no one is talking about their personal struggles, so we learn to suffer in silence. It is only through taking risks and talking honestly about ourselves that we can be free. Without honesty, all work is in vain. So, *to thine own self be true.*

Let's buckle-up and get ready to take a ride through the life of an EMOTIONAL PRISONER: TRAPPED BEHIND THE BARS OF MY THOUGHTS.

PART ONE

EMOTIONAL SET UPS THAT SET ME BACK

1

EMOTIONAL PRISONER

WHAT IS AN EMOTIONAL PRISONER? Emotional prisoners are people who allow all their decisions to be made by how they feel emotionally. When we talk about feelings, there are two ways we feel. The first is with our emotions and the second is by our instincts. Feeling by emotions is very unpredictable and feeling by instincts is predictable because it's God talking. Emotions talk to the mind as doubt, worry, and fear. Instincts show up as *a gut feeling* or what we call *our first mind*. To live by our instincts means we have to trust God. What does it mean to trust God?

First, we must take our mental hands off of our lives; we must relax and know that God has us covered. Second, we must not worry about our next move because we will know which way to go when it's time. Last but not lease we must learn to experience life and stop trying to control it. Control is an illusion.

Let's define emotion. Emotion is a part of consciousness (or the mind) that involves feelings or sensibility.

Now, let's define the mind. The mind is the consciousness that controls mental and physical behavior.

If we let part of our mind control our whole mind, our mental and physical behavior will be controlled by how we feel emotionally. The balance in our lives between what we feel and what we know to be right is not there; reason takes a back seat. The thing to keep in mind when we talk about emotions is that they're energy in motion, so when our emotions change, we change. They are never the same at all times and that's why it feels like a roller coaster ride when they are in charge – mentally up one minute and down the next. An emotional prisoner becomes locked into this mental cycle of ups and downs.

Now, let's define prisoner. A prisoner is one who is deprived of freedom of action or expression. Notice I did not say someone in jail. If you are not able to have freedom of action or expression, you are a prisoner. If it is your emotions that deprive you of freedom of action or expression, you are an emotional prisoner. We can never have freedom of action or expression when our lives are controlled by our emotions. The reason is that we will make our decisions based on how we feel; not on what we know is right for us at the moment. It is a fact that we feel, but feelings are not always the facts. That is to say, just because we feel something doesn't mean it is the truth. Emotions will, and often do, lie to us.

I've spent most of my life mentally trapped behind my feelings. As a result of their unpredictability, I became *strung out* on any and every thing looking for relief. I ended up helpless, hopeless, homeless, and addicted to crack cocaine. I became that guy begging you for change in front of the 7-11; my days were spent sitting at the bus stop picking up cigarette butts. I went from making almost $1,000 a week, to being reduced to a duffel bag full of clothes stuffed into a locker at the Greyhound bus station. I know what it feels like to lose everything and, out of all the things I lost, I missed my mind the most. My emotions had taken over my mind so completely that I could not make a rational decision to get some help. I had truly lost my mind and all sense of right and wrong. I lived a life full of insanity.

When emotions take over, there is no freedom of action or expression; it is all about how I feel. No one—not even me—understood the connection between emotion and addiction. Addictions are emotional outlets a way of escape from reality. I've never had an addictions problem but a *never wanting to feel bad problem*. Never wanting to experience the painful side of life leads to addiction. So I worked on the *symptoms (the addictions) and never* the emotional *problems*.

We tend to look at the symptoms and not the behavior as the problem. Others thought that if I could just stop smoking crack cocaine that would solve all my problems. How wrong they were. Crack cocaine was never the problem *it was the excuse I used* not to deal with my problems. I am an addict, but *José is my problem*. I am my own worst enemy. Crack cocaine was but a manifestation of my problems. Manifestation means that *the problem started from the unseen* – deep down within my soul.

If crack cocaine was the problem, how is it that I gained 70 pounds after I stopped smoking it? I gained 70 pounds as a direct result of eating to my emotions. I went from the crack house to the steak house; food had become my number one painkiller. I don't always eat because I'm hungry; I eat because I'm bored or hurting. I can remember getting out of the shower one day and as I passed the mirror, I almost went into shock at what I saw. I had become so big that I could not tell the back from the front and at that moment, I decided to do something about it. The only thing that will defeat emotions is action...the ability to act regardless of how I felt.

Since I have been sober from drugs, I have filed for bankruptcy because of shopping to my emotions. My emotions would tell me to go to the mall and spend the money for bills. On the way out, my mind would say, "You know you should have paid that bill." Remember, *emotions are energy in motion*; so they have great power to influence our ability to make rational decisions. A rational decision is made when listening to our *first mind* – God. An emotional decision is made when debating or second-guessing it.

I decided to file bankruptcy because I had A-1 credit but I was losing my sanity trying to hold onto the image I created through the things I purchased. Here, I am trying to convey that, as long as emotions are in charge, our lives will always be inconsistent.

Because I continued to ignore the emotional traps in my life, I started buying sex to relieve my negative emotional energy. As a result, I bought Herpes. I did not catch Herpes; I bought it by going to the places where it was being sold. It was never about the sex; rather it was about trying to change the way I felt. In my attempt to feel good, I ended up feeling bad, so now I have an additional problem on top of the original one that made me buy sex in the first place.

This stuff I am sharing is not for shock value – it is for freedom value. I don't care about shocking anyone. My mission is to help someone get free. This is not about me freeing me from you, but about me freeing me from my emotions. The purpose of emotions is to be a part of our lives, not to run our lives. The purpose is to allow us to feel love, compassion, joy, pain, sadness, gladness, and a host of other things that are a part of life. How could we truly know what *love* felt like if we didn't have emotions? Our goal here is not to control them or let them control us, but learn to experience our emotions as a part of life. We need to stop avoiding the painful emotions while only accepting the pleasurable ones. They all have their place in life; so learn to experience them all.

2

CREATING THE PRISON

I BELIEVE IT IS important to understand how the emotional prison is created. Without knowing *how* it is created, how can we know what keys to use for freedom? The lock is mental. The emotional prison is not a place; but a state of mind and the bars of the cell are the thoughts we choose because of what we believe. We don't get out of life what we want but what we believe at the core of our being. The door is shut behind us and locked once negative information becomes negative beliefs. The only way to be paroled from the prison of our minds is by seeking new information about the world and us, then acting upon that new information. Because information without application leads to frustration, having the knowledge and *not acting on it* causes mental frustration. The bars of the cell are created in our childhoods by the words and actions of others who, unknowingly, lock us up without our permission. As children, we are not capable of taking care of ourselves, so we depend on others. If *they are emotional prisoners*, how can we expect to be free? For this reason, we must start at the beginning of our lives so that we might see *why* we do what we do in the now.

Most people live their lives like the girl who watched her mother cook a ham. She noticed that her mother cut the ends off of the ham, so she asked her mother *why*. Her mother said, "Because my mother cut the ends off." So, the girl decided to call her grandmother to ask *why* she cut the ends off of her ham, and her grandmother said, "Because my mother cut the ends off." Finally, the girl called her great-grandmother to ask *why* she cut the ends off of her ham. Her great-grandmother said, "Honey, I cut the ends off because the pan was too small."

The question I propose to you is: *How long do you continue to cut the ends off of your life because somebody else's pan is too small?* We need to begin to question some things we were taught, and stop doing them if they're not working and learn something new. There must be a willingness to question everything we know because traditions keep me *stuck on stupid* for a long time. Visualize the title, EMOTIONAL PRISONER TRAPPED BEHIND THE BARS OF MY THOUGHTS. Stop for a moment and create the picture in your mind of you sitting in a jail cell. Now, picture yourself opening the door and telling yourself you're free. How does it feel? This is what this book is all about – helping you to free yourself from the prison of your mind where the jailer is your emotions.

One problem I see with "freedom" is that if it has not been experienced, we get comfortable with prison life. It is just like a person who has committed a crime, goes to jail, and gets *mentally institutionalized* from spending too much time locked behind bars that they become conditioned to serve time. The same is true for an emotional prisoner. The emotional prisoner becomes *emotionally institutionalized* because of spending so much time locked behind the bars of their thoughts that they also learn to "serve time" in life. Many of us have never truly experienced mental freedom because we were locked up at an early age; so we talk freedom instead of walking free. My mouth will say anything but my actions speak the loudest. In order to be free, the pain of staying the same has to become greater than the pain of changing. It is all painful except one is freedom and the other is bondage.

I am reminded of a story about an old man sitting on his front porch. The dog sitting next to him was constantly hollering. One of his neighbors walked by and asked, "Why is the dog hollering so much?" The old man replied, "He's sitting on a nail." The neighbor said, "Why doesn't he get off of it?" And the old man replied, "The pain is not great enough yet." The moral of this story is that when the pain gets great enough in your life, will you stop hollering and do something about it. Change is hard but resisting change is even harder. Change is a process and not an event that happens once it's a lifetime journey. This is why we must understand our beginning before we can change our end.

I did not start to dislike myself when I smoked crack cocaine. I started very early in life as a small boy who was teased and called names. The emotional pain caused by those actions led me into addiction because I was looking for a way to relieve myself of the negative energy. When I look back on my life, I was a prime candidate to be hooked on something. I would have gotten "hooked on phonics" if you told me it would change my mood. *My primary mission in life was to feel good all the time.* It wasn't until I lost everything that I became willing to go back to the beginning and try to see where things went wrong.

If we are not willing to hurt, we are not willing to heal. Truth be told, it has always hurt but we found ways to suppress it. This is where addiction runs rampant in our lives – trying to release a spiritual problem through physical means.

What are some of the signs that our lives are being controlled by our emotions?

One is procrastination, which shows up as low energy and a high desire to change. We really want to change our lives, but the mental and physical energy needed are not there; so we just give in to our emotions and struggle. Procrastination was so strong in my life that I bought a book on procrastination…I just haven't read it yet. All jokes aside, procrastination is a sign that our emotions are in the driver's seat of our lives and there must be a mental seat change of control if we plan to be free. Spirit must sit in the seat of control if we are to live a life that is guided – not one that is aimless. When we let emotions rule our lives, we become like leaves in the wind – whichever way the wind blows, that's where we will go.

Another sign is massive complaining all the time, which is dissatisfaction with our lives while we do nothing to change it. Complaining doesn't change anything but our attitude. We complain because it is easier than changing.

In the next chapters, I will show you how to solve the problem and live a life worth living. I will share with you how someone – who grew up without love, without encouragement, without a Father, and sometimes a Mother; someone who went through years of hell on earth of his own making – *chose* to make a winning life. This is my story of how I decided to look up, get up, and shape up mentally. I am living proof that – no matter how much you are in despair and no matter how challenging life appears to be – *you can overcome* your childhood to achieve victory in your life. *I did* and *you can* too. It only takes an honest desire to tell the truth, first to you; then to others. Then, develop a willingness to take positive action on those truths.

Life is a drama that can be rewritten *if we choose to* by getting to the root – the exact nature – of the emotional problems that are deep-seeded within each of us. So, here we go…keep an open mind. It may prove to be a rough ride but, in the end, it is a ride worth taking!

3

I'M A LIE

IT'S NOT THE LIES I tell but the lies I live. It doesn't matter what lies I tell you – it's the ones I keep telling myself.

Because we grow up in a world full of liars, we tend to follow the beaten path and become liars ourselves. What makes us all liars? We become liars the moment we lie about how we felt as a child when pain and discomfort was our lot.

I cried a lot as a young boy. Because I was slapped upside the head and called a "momma's boy," I began to lie about how I felt to avoid further abuse. The thing about lying to yourself is that it will show up somewhere else in your life. For me, I started wetting the bed. Because of the beatings I got for it, I began hiding the wet sheets and the lies continued. I was not allowed to show my emotions freely. I continued to lie about my feelings and, as a result, I became emotionally disconnected from myself.

As a child, I remember playing touch football in the street. I would run out for a pass, focusing so hard on catching the ball that I did not see the parked car. *Crash*…into the bumper I would go. All of my buddies would run over and one would ask if I was okay while another would say "get up and shake it off." This is where *I began living another lie*. I said I was all right but I was hurting. I got up and began to "shake it off" because I wanted to show them I was tough. Even today, I find myself getting hurt but try to act like I'm all right by shaking if off…never dealing with the hurt. I can only "shake off" but so much hurt. In time, the accumulation of pain will make me mentally sick.

When we lie about how we really feel, we cover it up with a lie on our face and out of our mouths. Lies cause internal pain and pain needs to release itself; so addiction "fills the bill."

Becoming a lie is a process that starts in our childhoods and become a way of life as adults. If allowed to go unchecked, they will destroy us. Here are some of the lies that I lived that I knew were lies but, because they had become a way of life, it was hard to let go?

For me, acting like a good church member but buying sex to quiet the pain in my mind of the lie I am, then going back to church and crying to Jesus about how sorry I am that I did that. Jesus can't stop my bad behavior; I have to help myself and stop living that lie. Another lie was trying to be "the good son" while not having healed my mind of my anger toward my Mother from my childhood and taking out that pain on my wife. Lying to myself about having some "good friends" in my life but really knowing they were takers because I was giving as a result of my need for approval and acceptance. At times, hating the world but would continuously say how much I love to help others. Yes, I *acted* nice but, in essence, I was a very angry person who covered-up the anger with people-pleasing.

Do you see the lies we live and, because we live them for so long, *we become them*? This is the main reason why "the truth hurts." Telling the truth means we have to give up a part of our-selves. We all show the world "a front," which is all the roles we play to get through life. Lying to ourselves never gets us through…we just get by.

Because playing lots of roles and becoming those roles stops the growing process, we become *stuck* on the stage of life. Waiting for the next chance to *play our part* so that we might award ourselves an Oscar for best actor or actress in a living drama called life.

Lies keep the mind sick and truth is the antibiotic that heals it. It will be painful in the beginning but we must become willing to feel worse before we can feel better by confronting the lies we have become. This is where courage is needed because "telling the truth" leaves us *at risk* of losing some of the people currently in our lives. I would rather lose them, than to continue to lose myself in the lies. It is not about physical courage; rather, it is mental and emotional courage to confess with our mouths, live the truth, and accept the results of those truths. Lies have kept us sick for so long. Why not take a risk to gain peace of mind? When our insides are comfortable, I realize that there is nothing in this world that compares with peace of mind.

When I say, "stop living a lie," it's important to be in tune with the Spirit of God on the inside of us because it tells us when to speak and when to shut up. Be mindful of this because we may cause ourselves more pain by trying to be honest about every single thing to every single person. We live in a world full of liars where the truth is *abnormal* for many people and those people will hold it against you. This is why being *in tune with the Spirit* is important.

There are roles all of us must play because *that's just the way life is*, but it's important to stay true to ourselves while in those roles. One of the dilemmas of role-playing is that we become the roles and lose all sense of self. Living the truth means playing the roles but staying connected to how we feel at that moment. If I'm playing the role of employee and the supervisor calls a meeting and begins the meeting with jokes that are not funny, it is important not to laugh. When I'm in the role of Father and my daughter is trying to take advantage of my kindness, it's important to stand strong and endure her being upset when I say "no."

These are but a few examples of being a living lie and why we must work to break the cycle. To be honest with someone just to clear my conscience while making him or her feel bad in the process is not what I'm talking about. What I am saying is to live in truth through awareness of the moment so that we might change the things we don't like about ourselves. The lies that kill are the lies we live.

Remember, God will only reveal the problem. It is up to us to take action.

4

SELF-INVESTIGATION

SELF-INVESTIGATION is taking inventory of our belief system to see what beliefs we have on the shelf of our minds. This is the first step toward fixing our bankrupt lives. Many of us *filed* spiritual *bankruptcy* when we gave up on our God-given potential by settling for less. We allowed the opinions of others become our reality.

Inventory means; to make an appraisal of, as in one's skills or personal characteristics. We must examine those beliefs we've held on our mental shelf to see what's good and what's not. Taking inventory is a fact-finding opportunity. The difference between a business inventory and the inventory we take on ourselves is that the business can *throw away* what's old and replace it with something new immediately. In taking a personal inventory, we must *work* the old ideals out of our minds by continuously feeding our minds new information.

The word "self," as used in the context above, means *the me that you don't see...the me* who cries on the inside but smiles on the outside as if everything is all right. The beliefs that worked as a child have become a ceiling to our spiritual growth in adulthood.

Self-investigation is digging into our past, so that we might have a future. It is not a search for blame; rather, it is a search for understanding of others so that we might better understand ourselves. "The others" are everyone who has interacted in our lives – from our mothers, fathers, siblings, and relatives, to the teachers, pastors, friends, and neighbors.

Why must we look at our *first* relationships? We must look because all of these relationships impacted the development of our belief system. What you believe is what you get out of life. Every person is a law unto him or herself. We set the rules for our lives by what we believe. God cannot free us from *the jail of our minds* if we're not willing to do the mental and emotional work necessary to be liberated.

I think a life that has not been investigated is a life not worth living. It is not worth living because *it's not your life* but merely a reflection of all of the relationships you've had thus far. Self-investigation will help us uncover to discover so that we can recover from the pain of our past that lives in our present moment through our minds, snuffing out all hopes for a future.

Life is happening *right now*. There is no tomorrow because when tomorrow comes it will be *right now* again. The emotional prisoner sacrifices "right now" by mentally living in yesterday or waiting for tomorrow hoping it will bring something new. However, the emotional prisoner fails to realize that, in order to get something new out of life, we must become someone new.

When I wrote my autobiography, I found that the only thing that changed about me was my age and my shoe size. I was a grown kid. Physically I grew but mentally and emotionally I stayed in a childish state. The autobiography was simply a *garbage run* to find out what stinks in my life. The real work comes in *putting out the trash*.

We were all created to bring something to this world and leave it here before we leave. It's called a purpose." We cannot get to our purpose until we deal with our pain. Our purpose has always been in us but we've piled so much pain and bad information on top of it until it can't get out. This is why we must investigate self – we must remove and get rid of the obstacles that block our awareness from seeing the true meaning of our lives. It is important to understand that it's going to hurt; however, this is "necessary pain."

There's a story about a guy who lost his keys in his house but decided to look for them outside. His friend came by and asked, "What are you looking for?" And he said, "My keys." The friend said, "Where did you lose them?" And he said, "Inside the house." His friend replied, "If you lost them in the house, why are you looking for them out here?" The guy's response was, "Because there's more light out here." The moral to this story is that the keys to the prison of our minds will not be found in the light of the world, but in the darkness of our souls. As long as we keep looking into the mirror of the world to see ourselves, we will only get back distorted images of who "they" think we should be. It's not until we look within will we find the true answers for our lives.

Now let's take a ride with *your eyes* into the life of *this* emotional prisoner. See if you find out something about yourself from my story. I'm not trying to impress, depress, or suppress; just to express my story. I will expose things about myself that may make you feel uncomfortable. Please do not mentally shut down, but read on. Here I go!

I was raised in a family that did not know how to be a family, so I was screwed up before I grew up. When I left home, I connected with other screw-ups, so it was easy for me to self-destruct. I was born in an era where providing the necessities was construed as love. I now know it's not the same thing. To a child, love is spelled "T I M E." If we don't spend time with our children, they internalize that as not loving them. Believe it or not, adults spell love the same way too. There's a difference between *providing for* and *raising* a child. Providing means that we pay the bills. Raising means nourishing the mind so it will grow to become mentally and emotionally able to handle life. Parenting is the most important job on the face of the earth because it's the process by which "the seeds" – our children – either blossom or become weeds. The tragedy is that parenting is *on-the-job training*. If the parents don't learn the difference between "providing for" and "raising," how will our children know when they become parents? Adults cannot teach what they do not know and this is how the vicious cycle continues.

I have chosen to take the risk by exposing my childhood so that you might see the emotional set-ups that set me back and work to avoid them in your life.

Because of the situation I was born into with no Dad, and my Mother having to make a decision to stay home and raise us or go to work to feed, shelter, and clothe us, I was *provided for;* not raised. Life doesn't give any breaks because we are mentally and emotionally *malnourished.* There isn't any mental or emotional welfare system to get on. Life was not – and is not – emotional, compassionate, warm, or gentle…people are. Life doesn't care about you or me – it has its own agenda and neither you nor I can interrupt or change that agenda.

I was what people called "a scratch baby." Everything I've done in my life I started from scratch. My Mother was in the hole, so I was in the hole too. When I was born, the doctor slapped me on the behind and I got up and went to work. That lets you know how long I've been working.

My siblings and I spent a lot of time alone at home. We were *latch key kids*. There was always someone there to beat me but no one there to teach me. The beatings were a way to instill fear in us to *do the right things* while they were gone. They were gone often. As a result of the beatings, I learned to respond to fear and not love. If somebody told me they loved me, it felt very uncomfortable…so uncomfortable to the point it made me look for ways to escape. When people told me they loved me, I took advantage of them. On the other hand, people who abused me I bowed down to them. If you instilled fear in me, I would probably do what you needed done before you asked.

Growing up, I can't remember being told by my parents that I was loved or that I was special. There wasn't much hugging going on in my house.

The first time I started receiving hugs regularly was when I became an alcoholic and attended *AA* meetings. In the beginning, it felt funny. I have since learned that hugs are very important because they connect our spirits. Hugs are food for the soul. Life was very difficult for me as a young boy because I was shy, afraid, and very emotional. I would cry if you hollered at

31

me...you didn't have to hit me – just holler. Because I was teased, slapped up-side my head, and told to "stop the whining," I learned to suppress my feelings early in life. To avoid the teasing and being slapped on the head, I stopped crying on the outside, but continued crying on the inside; so, *I never stopped crying.* I believe that as a child, if I could have cried more on the outside, I would have drank alcohol and done drugs a little less. Crying is an emotional outlet. Because I was not allowed to wash my face with tears to cleanse my soul of pain, I ended up self-destructing in an attempt to release that pain.

Suppressing my emotions created some problems. I did not know how to identify what I felt or how to deal with the negative energy so I reverted to "the familiar" – anger was the way I began expressing myself. Anger was not the problem – hurting was. Because *I did not know how* to express hurt, anger was the next best thing. Some people thought I might grow up to be "gay" so they set out to change that by punching me in the chest in their attempt to "make me hard." They didn't make me hard; what they did was to disconnect me from my emotional self. I was emotionally numb. I would rather have been gay and free than to be straight and stuck.

We do two things with our emotions: we either express them or suppress them. I became a suppressor. Suppression was *the norm* in my house and in my neighborhood because expression was taken as "talking back" and the wrath would come on you like a thief in the night. *Children were seen and not heard.* Children had no opinion about anything. With all the suppression in my young life, I became like a keg of dynamite in a hot room and all I needed was a spark to set me off. The thing about suppressing feelings is that a person cannot continue to do it without getting mentally and emotionally sick. For me, the pain showed up as wetting the bed. That was a sign that something was going wrong in me. No one knew anything about the mental and emotional aspects of life; so they tried to solve a spiritual problem with a physical remedy.

The physical remedy was to beat me when I wet the bed hoping that would make me stop. If beatings worked, I should be an Angel. The thing is that the insides cannot be fixed from the outside *unless* one is working on the insides from the outside. To use fear and abuse only creates more problems. My solution to avoid getting beaten was to change the sheets before anyone knew. I got good at avoiding the punishment but I never learned to solve the problems. Washday was early every Saturday morning and I would volunteer to wash the clothes by myself to cover-up the wetting and the neighbors thought I was being a good son.

When I went outside to play, children teased me about my name, José. They called me "Ho" for short. I didn't like that but I didn't like to fight either; so I swallowed the pain and took the abuse. My name caused me a lot of mental and emotional problems; the biggest problem was self-hatred. Some of the meanest people in the world are children because they will make you not like yourself. The teasing and name-calling were perpetuated when I did not have positive reinforcement at home. The only information I got about myself came from other children. My Dad wasn't around and neither was my Mother because she had to work all the time. I had no one to turn to in time of need. My defense mechanism to survive the teasing and name-calling was to become a "people-pleaser." I believed that if I made you my friend, you wouldn't tease or hurt me anymore. That worked for a while until others began to perceive me as being weak. When weakness is perceived as your dominating quality, get ready to be abused.

School was traumatic for me as well. There was one guy who abused me through Elementary and Junior High. He took my money and my lunch whenever he felt like it. Because of how this *one person* treated me, not only was I afraid of him, I became fearful of people in general. When I saw him coming down the hallway at school, I would slip into the bathroom until he passed. I always found ways to avoid confrontation and dealing with my problems. (Even today, it is hard for me to speak up and stand for what I believe in but it's gotten better with practice.)

As a child, I constantly felt powerless and mentally trapped by helplessness and hopelessness. To top it all off, I was a smart kid who made the Honor Roll but did dumb things to fit in with the crowd. I grew up in a community where to be smart made you a nerd and an outcast but to get shot and survive or go to jail made you a hero. In my neighborhood, to be called "crazy" meant you weren't to be messed with. My entire community was insane and to settle for less was the norm. It was a place where to succeed meant you became the *First National Bank of Hoodville*, where folks thought you should take care of their needs.

When I look back at my life, I see that I never made the human connection. I did not connect with my Father or any other man. My connection to my Mother was one driven by insanity. I did not connect with my brother or my sister because they played with their friends and I played with mine. There were no animals in the house because my Mother had asthma that was agitated by animal hair. In looking back, I had no connection with the people I called "friends" because of my disease to please. I bought all my "friends" because of the level of self-hatred that said *I'm not good enough*. I was always the first one to volunteer to pay for the drinks and the drugs, usually putting up more than my fair share.

Do you see the emotional set-ups early in my life that set me back as an adult? Back then I didn't know anything about mental and emotional pain, but I knew I was hurting and needed relief. And here comes sex into my life, introduced to me by a relative who also needed relief from the stress of growing up.

She wasn't wrong and I wasn't wrong. We were just curious and, because it changed how I felt, I became a sex addict at a very young age. I can remember finding some *X-rated* magazines and guarding them with my life like I found a pot of gold. I would sneak outside and go under the house to have an extended peek session. Over a period of time, just looking at pages of naked women got old and I needed something else to feed my sex addiction. That something else was looking through the keyhole in the bathroom door to watch the females in the house use the toilet or take a bath. I could be doing something but, as soon as a female went into the bathroom, I dropped whatever I was doing to get a peek because my addiction did not take any days off. I am sure there were times those women felt someone on the other side of the door because they would put a piece of toilet paper in the hole. I would push it out while they sat on the toilet. Addiction is so powerful that risk taking is not a risk at all. All of this is happening to me between the ages of 6 and 9 years old. I was sick at a very young age. There is no age requirement for mental and emotional illness.

Peeking through the keyhole was no longer satisfying and I needed something else to quiet my addiction. (Remember, addictions are emotional outlets; they are attempts to release negative energy.) I began riding my bike through the park. I would ride close to women who were jogging and grab their butts or breasts in an effort to feed my addiction. It didn't matter that some of the women would run me down, throw me off the bike, slap me around, and choke me half to death. I would get up, dust myself off, and look for another victim. I had no idea that the real victim was me.

Emotional pain left untreated gets more and more insane through addiction. It is important to talk about things that are uncomfortable because shared pain is eased pain and pain unshared yields a distorted life. It's much easier for a group of people to carry a load than for one person to do it alone. I tried to carry my mental baggage all by myself and it almost killed me.

We must go all the way back to the beginning where all of our relationships started. Our first relationships are how our belief system gets created. Once created, it becomes a way of life. Those first relationships keep repeating themselves throughout our lives. The relationships we had with others and the one we have with ourselves must be investigated.

One of the most dominant relationships in my life was the one with my Mother. This is the hardest part to talk about but the truth must be told if mental freedom is to be achieved. We live in a society where Mothers are held in high esteem; so to openly call things the way they are, and not the way they seem to be, takes courage. I remember talking about my mother in a 28-day drug treatment program and a guy wanted to fight me because of my story. He thought I should not talk about my mother openly. I love my mother, but *I didn't like her*. I did not like the person she was because of her attitude. My relationship with my mother was very confusing and full of insanity because of her own mental illness that she denied. I did not like the way she treated my brother or me because of her anger toward men – my father, specifically. My mother brought guys in to stay with us. Everything was fine as long as the men were working and, as soon as the money stopped coming in, they were on their way out. *Everything revolved around giving her some money*. When my brother and I worked, we had to give *all of our money* to my mother. My sister gave what she wanted to give. I began noticing the *double standard* early in life. The men who came into our house did not come into *our lives*. They wanted to be with my mother—not her children. Those men were made to feel like kings, as long as they paid the bills. When I dropped out of school in the 8th grade *nobody said* "go back." She told me to get a job. That reinforced my belief that it was all about the money. I internalized that into *a belief* that my Mother's only concern was "getting paid," and that women were gold diggers, only after a man's money. As a teenager armed with that belief, I set out on a mission to get women before they got me. Throughout my life, I've destroyed some great relationships because of that kind of thinking.

It wasn't until I crashed and burned from smoking crack cocaine was I willing to look at my whole life – not just my drug life. I'm glad I had that experience because it made me change and that would not have happened otherwise because I thought I was all right. The anger I had toward my Mother I took out on all women who got into a relationship with me. I abused women trying to get back at my mother for the way she treated me. It wasn't until I decided to deal with the source of my pain that I was able to break free from the shackles of my past. I had to confront the anger I had at my mother in order to respect and love my wife.

When I talk about confronting my mother, it was not in a *blaming* way but in a way where I refused to let her mistreat me. I was willing to speak openly about how I felt to others and, because it made them feel uncomfortable, they made excuses for her behavior. One of the excuses made was that my mother did the best with what she had. That's just not good enough. It still doesn't solve my "anger" problem that turned into mental and emotional illness and abuse of women. There can't be any forgiveness unless there is some level of mental healing. It was hard to forgive when I was still hurting and *not* calling things the way they were but how I wanted them to be. I never had the opportunity to be a child when I was supposed to be a child because I became my Mother's husband – trying to be the "man of the house." Because my mother said that she should have put us up for adoption, I *decided* to carry that load. At that moment, I thought it was my fault for the way her life turned out so I set out to change that by working at a very young. I didn't want it to be my fault that she was unhappy. I carried an adult load on a child's back and the weight was too much to bear. *Now,* I realize she made that statement because of her own mental and emotional frustration with life.

Now let's talk about my Father, a guy who I saw from time to time when it was time to give up some money. He never had time for me. I am named after him but that's about all I got from him. This will be short and sweet because there's not much to talk about. I need to bring it up to show you how *not being there* can still cause pain in life. Neither my Father nor my uncles saw a need to be in my life, so I did not learn how to bond with men. I have a hard time today connecting with other guys. It was not important in my life because it wasn't important to my father and uncles. You see, the first things learned are the hardest to change. I have to force myself to call other guys if I want to grow in that area of my life. This is yet another emotional setup that set me back. I had anger for my mother who made me hate women and I did not connect with men because of my father. The result was that I became a loner who did not like to be alone. All of this happened before I was a teenager. At the age of 13, alcohol was introduced into my life and I thought I had found the answer to help me exist.

For a while, alcohol allowed me to be comfortable in my own skin. I was not all right when I was with others and I wasn't all right when I was by myself. Shortly afterwards, marijuana (weed) slipped into my darkness as another means of escape from the prison of my mind.

Most of my life I lived on welfare but I wasn't faring well. The pressure kept building up in my mind and, at the age of 14, a pipe burst. I was hospitalized for hypertension with a fever of 105. Think about the diagnosis – *hypertension*. The tension in my life went from normal to hyper and it showed up in my body. The stress of living almost cost me my life. Most physical illness can be traced back to mental illness but few doctors

43

treat the mind; they just write us another pre-scription. We live in a pill-popping society. We take pills to live with our problems; we never learn to solve them.

By the age of 16 going on 17, I decided to join the U.S. Army with a buddy on the buddy plan. When it came time to sign up, "my buddy" changed his plans. I went anyway. Going into the Army was an attempt to escape my environment. I did not know that my environment was a part of me; I take me everywhere I go. While in the Army, my alcoholism went to the extreme. I *hated* being hollered at and the hollering led me to drowning my pain with a drink. Hollering mentally caused me pain as a child and I was too big to cry; so I talked back and got into trouble. Remember, as a child I cried if someone hollered at me. My mother's constant fussing and hollering drove me crazy – literally. See how something from our childhood still affects us as adults? If you want to make me mad just start hollering at me.

I decided to get out of the Army before they put me out with nothing but a bad discharge. I went back home feeling like somebody, all decked out in my Army greens and my patent leather shoes. Everybody was patting me on the back and all the girls wanted to marry me because they thought I was somebody. That lasted until my money ran out; then I became *just José* again – the dishwasher and busboy.

One day I decided to pack my bags and head east to Washington, DC, to live with a buddy I met in the service. While in DC, I went on my search for fame and fortune, not knowing that, without knowledge of self, I would self-destruct. I began to act out on my sex, alcohol, and drug addictions until everything came to a screeching halt. I was left with a person I did know – me. The end result was being helpless, hopeless, homeless, and addicted to crack cocaine. It is what I call "hitting the wall," and it was at that wall I had my spiritual awakening. Finally, I realized and accepted the truths about my life.

Physical defeat often brings spiritual awakening because everything outside of us must stop working before we are willing to look inside of ourselves for the answers. For me, it was going to a drug treatment facility *four times* before I got it right. It is important to understand that, if you don't *continue to try to stop,* you will never learn *how* to "stay stopped." This is true for all addictions.

Because the treatment center gave me some insight into my real problems, I decided to go into therapy. While in therapy, I was prescribed all kinds of *mind medicine* just to make me mentally functional. My mind was so messed up that I would get depressed for weeks, and suicide would begin to be an option for me. I would be driving across a bridge and thoughts of going through the guardrail would come into mind.

Today, I am not on any medication for depression. This is a direct result of healing my mind from the pain of my past. Therapy didn't change my life; it showed me what needed to be changed *in my life* because I was honest by sharing the whole story.

Many people go into therapy concerned about *what the therapist thinks;* so they share some of the stuff – not all of it. Freedom must be an all-out truth-telling adventure that will leave you hurting in the beginning but free in the end. It is only through exposing those deep dark secrets of the past that will allow you to be mentally free. Because once somebody knows about them, other than just you, it's not a secret anymore. *We are all as sick as our secrets.*

I did not want to talk about peeking through the bathroom keyhole to watch my mother bathe or use the toilet, or how the first person with whom I had sex on a regular basis was a relative. I did not want to give details about riding my bike through the jogging trail solely to grab women's butts and breasts. But *I had to talk about it* because I did not want to smoke crack cocaine anymore. Telling it all was the only way out. The mental freedom I enjoy today was acquired *only by taking the risk* of getting gut-level honest and not be ashamed. I cared what others thought about me, but I did not care enough to stay sick. It took courage to talk and share honestly about myself, but this was my only road to freedom because *I was the biggest fake I knew!* It wasn't until I told the truth that I was able *to be me* all the time and in all places.

In order to be free, we must take a mental risk by telling it all and letting the chips fall where they may. Everybody, including therapists, should *get therapy* because we all have deep dark secrets that keep our life energy drained. Nobody goes through life without being touched by insanity…there are no untouchables. We all have problems that need our attention. Many of us go through life with something very important missing – knowledge of self. That void will determine whether we live or die mentally. We don't know our likes or dislikes because we are too busy being great *pretenders* – pretending to be somebody we're not. The work of self-discovery is one of pain and discomfort, so many of us would rather just close and lock the door to our past and throw away the key. But the past is a living, breathing energy that cannot be locked away. The past must be exposed to rid us of the baggage it carries. Our lives will not get better without our participation. We have to participate if we want our lives to change. God does not *drop from the sky* to change our lives because he gave us "free will" to change it ourselves. Take a look at *your life* and you will see that it is a mirror image of *your choices*. We must *choose to change* by making the hard decisions about our lives and God will give us the strength to go through. Change is simply doing something different about the same old stuff. We don't go through any new stuff; rather, it's the same old stuff day in and day out. Self-investigation will hurt; so, if you are looking for easy or soft truths this journey is not for you right now.

I had to confront the pain of my past so I would stop running from one addiction to another in my attempt to release it. It is not my childhood that caused me problems; rather, *it was the memory of my childhood* that caused me problems. Memories are thoughts with energy attached to them. What I mean is this: *Think of something* that was funny last week, last month, or last year. More than likely, you can still laugh at it today. Why? Because of the *positive energy attached* to that thought. That's why when someone dies we hold onto their memory. Memory is an energy that never dies – it can be felt forever. The same is true about painful thoughts that have *negative energy attached* to them. Because it hurts, we immediately try to push those thoughts out of our consciousness – but the thoughts remain in our *sub*conscious. By pushing them out of our conscious immediately, we neither deal with nor confront the pain so the negative energy cannot be released. It remains in our subconscious and continues to reappear. In time, the negative energy will turn into emotional problems.

We must get to know our pain so that we can release the negative energy attached to it. We burn a lot of mental energy running from our past so we end up tired and beat from the routine. If change were easy, everybody would do it. Usually anything easy will be where the masses are. Look at what everybody else is doing and do something different. The masses will always take the path of least resistance. There are not many who are willing to hurt in order to be healed. We want the benefits of being healed but are unwilling to do the work. The only place *reward* comes before *work* is in the dictionary. We must have patience with ourselves because this is a process and not an event. Changing our lives is not a destination; rather it is a journey filled with a variety of experiences. Change must be a way of life that must be adhered to every day because there is always room for improvement. The reason *change* is a lifetime journey is that, the more we learn, the more we know about ourselves. We have buried stuff so deep down in our minds that we have forgotten it happened. The more we dig into our past the more freed our minds will be until we get to a place where peace reigns.

5

THE EASY ONE

WHAT IS AN "EASY ONE"? "The easy one" is the one who is the easiest to take advantage of. If you're anything like me, consider yourself an easy one. We put everybody's needs ahead of our own, and believe it is important to be nice to everybody even if we dislike them. An easy one is the person other people call when they are in need because 9 out of 10 times the answer will be "yes."

Easy ones *always* say "yes" when we really want to say "no," but the fear of being disliked keeps us trapped. We put ourselves in a mental position where we think our family can't live without us, so we go through life trying to control and maintain every moment of life so others might be comfortable. Then, we become over-bearing to the point that others begin to dislike us. They begin to take us for granted and we begin to feel unappreciated. The feeling of being unappreciated forces us to re-evaluate those relationships, at which time we lie to ourselves by saying we will *only* take care of ourselves. This lie lasts about a day or two because we begin to feel guilty for taking care of ourselves while letting others fend for themselves.

I am so easy that complete strangers have taken advantage of me because I send out the message that I'm a pushover and just want to help. It doesn't matter whether or not I am a pushover to that person receiving the messages, the results are the same.

My need to please had become a sickness and I often found myself in a place of loneliness and despair. One thing I noticed is that I don't like people to dislike me so I go to great lengths to be nice. That saying, "He's nice to a fault," is true about me – and probably you – if you are an easy one.

Nice people don't finish last; we finish sick because *being nice has become a bad habit*. I go on for months taking care of everyone's needs while neglecting my own and, sooner or later, I hit *the wall*. The wall is an emotional breakdown resulting from me ignoring my mental, physical, and spiritual needs. People are hospitalized for emotional breakdowns. I am talking about the same kind of breakdown that can be as severe, but not to the point of hospitalization. I have what I call *mini breakdowns* where I "lose it" for a day or two. Once "I recover," I go back to doing the same things that broke me down in the first place. When I hit the wall, it makes me look at my life honestly. What I see is that I've been unhappy for a long time but continue to act as if everything is all right.

At the writing of this book I have pulled back from a lot of people, including some family members because I'm tired of being "the easy one." I have to force myself not to wash dishes or cook, even if it bothers me. I try not to always be home when everyone gets in because I fall victim to "the easy one" every time.

My wife and daughter went on a one-week trip and, while they were gone, I was stress free. As soon as they came back, I began to overeat. My wife got sick from headaches and sinus problems as soon as she walked in the door. I believe her illness came from thinking about my expectations of what I thought she should be doing, like cooking and cleaning more often. My illness came from the mental burden of taking care of them when just a day before I was stress free. It was like being on a vacation that was stopped abruptly to go back to work again. As "the easy one," I did not have a life of my own; rather, it was an illusion based on what I did for others.

Too often, *easy ones* try to live off of the praise and glory of others but deep down inside we are empty vessels. The crack house, jailhouse, churches, and mental institutions are filled with *easy ones*. We are the type of people who get mad with others, but hurt ourselves. We will not confront other people and situations that make us sick but rely on hope and prayer to "fix" those people or that particular situation. We hope and pray things will get better on their own, but that's not how life works. Hoping that people or things will change because we are nice is just wishful thinking and a waste of time and energy. "The easy one" is always tired because of the physical and emotional strain of taking care of everybody else, coupled with being unhappy and, at times, just sad. We can live with being unhappy for a while, but sadness will make us kill ourselves.

How do we change our lives from being an *easy one* to being a nice person who is not a wimp? We must set limits. We can still help others but without limits we will always overdo for others and forget ourselves. When we make our mental to-do list, we must put ourselves at the top of that list. If we put ourselves last, there won't be enough energy left to meet our needs and our needs are put "on hold" again. We put our needs on hold for so long that we don't know what we need anymore, but we know we need something.

I tried to meet my need for love through sex and my need for understanding through overeating. The first thing I had to do was to *feel the fear* of confronting others, accept it, and *do it anyway*. Confronting others, especially those who are closest to us, is a scary task. I get nervous and shake. My mind begins to play all the negative things that might happen as a result. If I see the results in my mind before I do it and those results are bad, more than likely I will not confront...I will stuff it. It's the *stuffing* that makes me sick. I have a choice – get better by confronting those people or stay sick by stuffing my feelings. Remember, if we allow fear to keep us from speaking out because we may lose someone, we still lose someone by keeping quiet – that someone we lose is usually us. The question is whether or not to *save face* at the cost of our lives, or *save our lives* at the cost of our face. Saving face is about faking and lying; saving our lives is about honesty.

When we confront others they will attempt to make us think we are losing our minds or are totally wrong in our views. This is where we must stay strong and committed to what we believe; otherwise, we will soften the truth to *save face*. I've had people reject and deny what I had to say as inaccurate or fussing. The problem with "the easy one" is that when we confront someone, we go back on our word and break the commitment we made to ourselves by taking care of others again. Our *actions* cause others to "take for granted" what we say because they know we don't mean what we say. I am a person who, when serious, I express it in a non-threatening way because I don't want to ruffle any feathers. What happens is that people will not respect what I say because they've heard me say it before. I begin to harbor anger and resentment toward my family, friends, and the world in general. If I keep treating people nice and they treat me like *crap*, I'm sending out the wrong message—I'm *showing* them that it's all right to walk all over me. *Turning the other cheek* has made my face sore. It's time to stop turning the other cheek and begin to speak up.

The second thing I had to do was to start being honest about how I really felt in my relationships. Most of my relationships were based on need, not honesty. I took a lot of *crap* because I feared that my needs would not get met. I spent eleven years people pleasing in my marriage, and now that I've worked on myself, it's hard for me to settle for anything less. When I changed, I began to dislike some of the people who were close to me. Being dishonest about the way things were going and letting them fester for a period of time meant a lot of discomfort for me when I spoke up. It has been an uphill battle because the people in my life got comfortable with "the easy one," and continued to resist *the new me*. I lost some people and removed others from my life because it was easier to start with new people who did not know the *old me*. I had to quit jobs as a result of being "the easy one" at work. I went to work trying to be everybody's friend and in the end felt used and abused. I *forgot* that the reason I went to work was to make money first and friends second – I was doing the reverse. "The easy one" always said "yes" to every assignment but got few raises. The awareness that I was an easy one at work was brought to light while working for Sprint PCS as a field tech. Once, while riding with another field tech, we began to talk. He told me that our supervisor said that he always asked me to do things because I never said "no." I was referred to as his "go-to guy" whenever he needed something done, no matter what hour of the day or night. At that moment, the truth of those words stabbed me in the heart like a sharp knife and penetrated my awareness like a bright light. The truth was so bright that it hurt my mind. At that moment I felt abused and misused but the reality was that *it was my fault* because *I chose* to be "the easy one" regardless of the needs I was trying to meet. If I volunteered for every assignment, if I went "the extra mile" and, in the end, I was left holding the bag of emotional sacrifice, it was *my choice*. Accepting that *I made a choice* kept me from looking for someone or something to blame. Nobody took advantage of me without my permission.

If we continue to make choices from what's happening on the outside of us then we suffer the plight of "the easy one." There must be an awareness of the voice from within that tells us to stop taking care of others and start taking care of ourselves. Staying "the easy one" will cause mental problems. Why would we keep hurting ourselves? It's time to change.

The third thing to break the habits of "the easy one" is to understand the law of mutual exchange. The law states that we give as we receive. The dilemma with this law for "the easy one" is that we give much more than we receive. I believe "the easy one" doesn't know how to ask for, or receive, what we need. We don't ask when we need something, because we expect people to know we are in need and we will say we're all right when we're not. The law states that we give as we receive.

Let's turn the law around and receive as we would give. This will be hard for a giver to receive before they give because of the habit of giving and taking care of others. And when we merge that with the teachings from the Bible on giving, it makes it a struggle. Struggle if we may but change we must, or die mentally and emotionally. There is no progress without struggle. When we are out of balance with this law we actually create our own problems while blaming others for them. *To give only* keeps us out of balance and we begin to feel victimized. Now, when we start to receive *before we give*, it will make us feel self-centered. "The easy one" doesn't want to be known as self-centered, even if we are. I believe everyone should be self-centered, not other-centered, especially "the easy one." "The easy one" is other-centered. Self only comes to mind when we have an emotional breakdown. When I talk about self-centered, I'm not referring to it as the world sees it. The self-centered person the world talks about is a taker and we don't need any more of them. The self-centered I'm speaking of is listening to the voice of guidance on the inside. Acting on that guidance will tell us what to do in all situations. The world is full of takers and givers, but very few *taker-givers* who are balanced people.

We are all here to be interdependent, not dependent on each other. We may need help from time to time, but we should not be a burden on someone else. Interdependent means we are responsible for our lives but we still have to learn to live together. When we are at either end of the mutual exchange spectrum we have become dependent not interdependent.

Takers are dependent people who need givers to stay alive. The problem with being a dependent taker is that valuable time is being wasted. In the long run, the givers leave and the takers are left "holding the bag." Many takers, as they get older, become locked into a way of life that actually destroys them. *Takers must start giving* – first to themselves by learning to be responsible for their lives. If they don't, as time passes their suffering will increase.

Now the givers are dependent too because they have caretaker issues. Givers need to take care of someone else to feel good about themselves. The givers need takers to survive because without takers who would they take care of? The giver believes that giving is more important than receiving but fails to realize that *giving* <u>and</u> *receiving* work together to create balance in life. Givers give more out of emotional need than love because they love to hear people say good things about them. The giver has to watch out for two personalities that drive their lives: *the Rescuer* and *the Victim*. The Rescuer comes out when anyone has a need, including total strangers. When they are in "rescue mode," they believe it's their job to solve everyone else's problems. Givers will do that at the expense of hurting themselves, even putting them in a financial hole. They don't want anyone leaving their presence without doing something nice. Yet, if they look at the decision making process, they will realize that everybody is right where they are supposed to be by choice. Now the Victim comes out when the Rescuer is burned out or hurting. Their cry is, "*Nobody seems to care*" or "*Why me?*" There's a saying that says, "Treat people the way you want to be treated." Givers work hard to live up to that statement – no matter what! When "the praise" stops or the *giving* is not reciprocated, the giver gets mad at the world and cries *victim*. It's not the world's fault, it's the fault of *the giver* who *chose* to be nice to everyone and give away all that they own.

If it were easy to stop being an easy one, there would be no need for this chapter. It is not easy to stop being easy. I've been easy much longer than

I have been firm. Old habits don't leave without a fight. Fight if we must, but "the easy one's" way of thinking and being has to go or we will never be free.

Last but not least, "the easy one" must look at life with honesty and clarity. We must call things as they are—not how we want them to be. I realized that with all my physical success I still didn't like myself so I spent lots of money trying to feel good. Of all the things I have changed in my life, learning to love myself has been the most challenging. I am not alone on this issue because I've spoken with many people who don't like themselves either. The world is full of self-haters. We try to cover it up by being successful materially but that only works when we are with others. The void and emptiness returns when we are alone with ourselves. We are *dressed-up garbage cans,* so full of crap that *it stinks* in other areas of our lives. Then we have children and they become *trash collectors*, collecting all of our mental and emotional garbage, and the cycle continues.

Today it's all about breaking mental and emotional cycles. *We can stop the madness.* "The easy one" must be dealt with at all cost if we expect to free ourselves from the prison of the mind.

Anger

Repressed anger is the number one cause of stress in our lives and stress produces all types of addictive behavior. The word *repress* means *to hold back*. Anger is defined as a feeling of great displeasure, hostility, indignation, or exasperation. Repressed anger is the feeling of great displeasure that we hold back or stuff deep within.

I was a stuffer, so my anger was always repressed and only let out through over using sex, food, shopping, gossip, etc.

As a young boy, I was not allowed to show my displeasure or anger. When it came out as an adult, it was of such magnitude and force that it scared me. That caused me to try to keep it locked up for life through suppression. I learned that no one could lock up anger; it has a key to the door of our minds and comes out without regard for others. Repressed anger drains us of all the energy of life until we become "the walking dead." It is important to begin to *constructively* express our displeasure with others, especially about the way they are treating us.

When I started expressing my anger with others, it felt physically uncomfortable. After the confrontation was over, mentally I felt great. I had to stop trying to control how it came out and just let it rip. There was not any physical violence because that would only make things worse and the problem is not resolved. If you are prone to violence, it is important to *get help first* before you pursue expressing your anger. When I say, "Let it rip," I'm talking about saying what you feel and, if there is a need to apologize, do it later.

I began expressing my repressed anger to my family and friends. They didn't like me as much—but I loved me more. When we don't express how we feel it turns into *people pleasing,* which makes others like us, but we begin to dislike ourselves. Self-hatred is like a fire inside of our house but we do not try to get out.

Another benefit of expressing my anger was my decline in self-destructive behavior. I don't destroy myself as much because I don't have a lot of pent-up negative energy to be released. All my life I was taught to repress – not express – my displeasure, so it turned into resentment. Resentment is anger that has been repressed which marinates in our minds for an extended period of time until it becomes pain. Pain not confronted becomes mental and emotional illness and hatred for others.

How do we express and not repress our anger?

There must be a willingness to take a risk of losing others in order to be free. We must not let the fear of someone packing up and leaving keep us locked into this cycle of pain. It is very scary for many of us to confront so we keep quiet; however, we fail to realize the futility in our own lives because we fail to speak out. Start with some small displeasures, such as not keeping the house clean, washing the tub, or cleaning up after themselves. As we gain strength from those expressions, go on to bigger ones like being unhappily married or friends who only call with their problems and you listening when you should be honest with them about their situations. We can't be honest with them about themselves until we get honest with us about ourselves.

We must stop repressing and begin expressing ourselves and watch how much our internal lives get better. There is a place in our lives for anger because, if we didn't get angry about something, change would not be possible. The problem comes from years of suppression until it becomes feared. One word of warning about expressing displeasure: our *physical* lives may suffer temporarily because of the wrath of others, but that is the price of freedom. Not to take a risk to be free is *choosing* to stay mentally in jail. The price may seem high at times but the reward is out of this world.

6

RELATIONSHIPS

THE REASON MANY OF US HAVE BAD RELATIONSHIPS with other people is that we have a bad relationship with ourselves. The real purpose of relationships is to help us find ourselves. If we have any hidden problems relationships will bring them out.

I attract and accept people into my life who match up with what I believe about myself. If I want my relationships to change for the better, I have to change for the better. If I have low self-esteem, I will choose people who are dominant. If I am dominant, I will choose people with low self-esteem to be submissive to me. I believe it is important not to be extreme in either, but to have balance between the two. Let's talk about self-esteem which is the relationship picker. We will choose our relationships based on how we feel about ourselves.

We hear people talk about self-esteem all the time but few really know what it means so we pass it around as a cliché. There are two parts to self-esteem: *self-concept* and *self-confidence*.

Self-concept is the way *I perceive myself* as I relate to others and the world. We must take a look at what we believe about ourselves because that's how we will act.

In my childhood, I was taught to feel inferior. I felt dumb and stupid most of the time in a world where I could not find a fit. My outlook on life made for a mental "ball and chain" existence where my mind was locked up in fear.

When people feel inferior no one has to tell them to sit in the back of the room; they will go automatically. People who feel inferior laugh at jokes that aren't funny, leave out of the side door, and do not speak up even when they have something good to say.

There are two ways to look at life: as a victim or a conqueror. People who feel inferior look at life through the eyes of a victim, they see the world as a scary place with a whole lot of bad people waiting to take advantage of anyone not mentally or emotionally strong. When we become victims, everything happens to us *not* for us. Because I did not have a good self-concept of myself, I was a *volunteer who cried victim*. Why me? I'm such a nice guy, I'm just trying to help, was my victim cry. When we have a bad self-concept we tend to give away more than we receive; we do more than necessary. Both rich people and poor people struggle with this issue because self-concept is developed in childhood.

Now, the second part is self-confidence, which is *how competent* we are when it comes to living. Can we take care of ourselves or do we need someone to hold our hands to keep us from falling? If we look at the trend in the world today we will see that many people need their hands held because they were never taught how to stand on their own two mental feet. There are more adults still at home in their 30's and 40's because it's a safe and secure place. There are more sons becoming their mother's husbands. There are many dreams that will not be realized because too many people are not confident enough to live them. We cannot make anything happen in this world if we do not believe in ourselves and act on that belief.

I was never taught self-confidence; rather, I was taught to doubt myself and fear the world. So how do we raise our self-esteem to become useful human beings? It's much easier to raise our self-confidence than it is to change our self-concept. Our self-concept is about who we are, and our self-confidence is about what we do.

Let's start with the easier one: *self-confidence.* When we raise our self-confidence it changes our self-concept. To raise our self-confidence, we must begin by finishing what we start. I'm a good starter, but a bad finisher. When I don't finish the things I start, it tears down my self-confidence. When I talk about finishing something, be it a book, cleaning the basement, or going back to school to complete a degree, it's important to understand that the objective is not *what I complete*, but *that I complete* what I start. Quitting is a habit but so is winning. It's hard to like ourselves when we quit all the time. People preach the philosophy of winning but fail to take into account that, *if it's not a habit, we won't win.* In order to build self-confidence, we must get better at completing the small things in our lives. It's never the blowout; rather, it is the slow leak that takes the air out of our lives and eventually we end up flat. Everything large in our lives started out small and grew out of not finishing. When we don't finish what we start, it leaves a memo stamped on our minds as "things to do." When we have too many unfinished things that come due at the same time, we feel overwhelmed and stressed.

The change for me was to finish cleaning the attic that I started cleaning four years prior. It felt great when I completed that task. Starting an exercise program to get in shape and writing a budget and sticking to it were some of the little things I did to build my self-confidence. When the toilet paper ran out, I put a new roll on the holder, not on the back of the toilet. This may seem trivial but it's how I created the habit to finish what I started. It's about follow through, not just doing enough to get by. Many people do just enough to stay alive but never enough to live. There is a difference between living and being alive. Living is doing *more* than what needs to be done and alive is doing *only* what needs to be done. We don't have to get everything right but we must get more right than we get wrong if we want to win. The percentage of winning decisions must outweigh the percentage of losing decisions.

Next is *self-concept*. This is hard to change because the first things learned are the hardest to change but it can be done. I am a living example. To change my self-concept I had to change the information I'd been operating on about myself. This is where the real work began and I remained consistent to drive out my old way of thinking.

The constant theme throughout this book is our beliefs and how everything is a reflection of what we believe. Beliefs are simply information we have internalized as the truth. Changing our self-concept will be a challenge because of the battle that will commence in your mind between the old you and the new you. In addition, there will be a struggle with others you used to bow down to and now you are speaking up and standing up for yourself. They will try to push you back into the box using anger, guilt, or love. People who are close to you know how to use love to manipulate you to stay where they perceive as your place in life. This is where listening to your "gut" will be important because you will be bombarded with external information coming from everywhere and everyone.

When I started standing up for myself and what I believed in, the people around me started feeling uncomfortable. They had become comfortable with the old me. But the old me was killing me and causing me lots of mental and emotional pain. There must be a willingness to risk losing something in order to win everything and everything is mental…it is peace of mind. As long as we fear losing, we will never do what's necessary to change our self-concept and win. We can know everything about ourselves but, without the ability to act on what we know, it's merely information about ourselves.

Change is very uncomfortable so we must get comfortable with being uncomfortable. As a result of taking life on and handling the hard challenges, I've become a person I like to be with all the time. The hard challenges may be at home where we stop taking a lot of crap from family and friends. We begin to confront, and let the chips fall where they may. We take entirely too much crap from people who are close to us and with whom we work. We must start at home with our family and friends because we have acted in a way that is pleasing to them but displeasing to us. Then, we must go to work and keep integrity with ourselves by staying true to what we believe in and stop holding it in so we don't rock the boat.

Of all the relationships I have, the most important one is the one with myself, so I advise that we stay true to ourselves in *all* roles.

7

ADDICTIONS

Addictions are emotional outlets and mental survival tools. Until we deal with our mental and emotional problems, addiction will always be a constant theme in our lives.

What is addiction? Addiction is the mental condition of being addicted, dependent upon, or habit-forming behavior. What does it mean to be addicted? To be addicted is to be controlled by things and/or behaviors that keep us stuck and are totally ruin our lives. Addictions are habits. Habits are recurring patterns of behavior acquired through repetition, often done without thinking. So an addict is a person who habitually gives to themselves, so that makes us all addicts.

We are under the illusion that addicts are people who use drugs, so many of us will miss getting the help we need because of this misconception. Today, we are addicted to everything – from the Lottery to the Lord. The problem is that we try to compare our addictions with one another in an effort to justify our habits by saying *I'm not as bad as so and so*. This comparison happens mentally most of the time. It's hardly ever verbalized. I found myself comparing my addictions by telling myself when I overate it was not as bad as smoking crack – as if it's all right to overeat. What's the difference between smoking crack cocaine and overeating? The difference is *time of destruction it will take me a little longer to kill myself.*

People who gossip think they're better off than the person who shops to their emotions. The *shop-aholic* thinks their better than the *sex-aholic*, and the *sex-aholic* thinks their better than the *alcoholic*. The *alcoholic* thinks their better than the *heroin addict*, and the *heroin addict* thinks their "a cut above" the crack cocaine addict. Crack cocaine addicts live at such a low level that we don't think we're better than anyone. We need to stop comparing and start understanding each other's addictions so that we might work together to help heal ourselves.

Addiction is the same hook but different bait. It's not *what I use* but *why I use* it. The bait is anything I use to change how I feel. It can be food, money, sex, drugs...the list is endless. The bait is never the problem; rather, *what I use* to avoid my mental and emotional problems. It's important to understand that the problem is the hook.

The hook is the behavior or desire for something – it is "lusting after." To lust doesn't necessarily mean sex; rather, it is a strong desire to have something at all cost. I can lust after money, food, fame, or anything. What drives the behavior is the mental obsession and the physical compulsion. A mental obsession is an idea, image, or emotion that occupies the mind continually. Simply put, it is *one thought that overpowers any other thought*. A physical compulsion is an irresistible urge or impulse. In other words, once I get started I don't know when I will stop.

As addicts, we are trapped by our need for instant gratification. Once the act is done it seems to be lacking fulfillment so we continue to repeat the same behavior hoping it might get good again because at one time it worked to relieve the pain. It's not the trap that killed the rat, but it was the love of the cheese. Just like the rat knew there was a trap, it still took the chance—

because of the love for cheese—and sacrificed its life. We do the same thing with our lives. What love of cheese are you willing to die for? The cheese can be sex and the trap HIV; or food and the trap is obesity to the point of becoming unproductive. Gossip – which is precious time in idle conversation – can be the cheese and the trap is wasting your life by talking down on someone. The cheese can be anything and the trap is what we get down the road. This trap and cheese analogy sounds cute but the real challenge is to change by understanding our addictions. We must know why we use whatever we use.

I don't know about you, but I didn't change my life because it was the right thing to do; I changed things because it hurt too much for me to stay the same. Everything I've changed has scratch marks on it. I didn't just let it go, I felt defeated and I quit. *It must hurt me* because *hurting my family was not enough* to stop me from doing whatever I did to destroy my life. Why did it take so much pain to let go? Because it was a habit and habits don't leave without a fight. Most addictions start out as pleasure or fun and, over time, turn into pain because of abuse. By then, it's too late because it's become a way of life. It is only through pain and suffering that we become willing to let go. Once something becomes a habit, it becomes a part of us, and stopping turns into an uphill battle for survival.

There are three stages to addictive behavior: *using, abusing,* and the *bottom. Using* is the first stage where it's fun; we're still functional at the level of humanity. If we have a job we can still go to work and hide our addiction. This is how the trap is set because it gives us what we're looking for—momentary relief from the drama we call life. Now, as we try to make it last for an extended period of time, we enter the second stage of addiction, which is *abuse.* In the abusing stage, we make our addiction the first thing in our lives. We put it in front of the things we should be doing. In this stage, we go from using for fun, to using out of need. We start to do crazy stuff to get our fix—whatever our fix is. We'll spend money at the mall to feed our shopping addiction and then try to cover the loss by re-working the bills. This stage can last for years until, after burning all the bridges in our lives, we are left with ourselves. This is the last stage – the *bottom.* The bottom stage is where we have gone as far as we need to go, and are now ready for a new direction in our lives. The bottom stage is where the addiction stops working to hide the pain. It actually causes us more pain on top of the pain we already have. With all addictions, we must hit *rock bottom* first, before we become ready to try something new. The bottom doesn't have to be a physical bottom—and usually it's not—it can be an emotional and mental bottom.

When I was homeless, it wasn't just the physical bottom that made me change, but the mental and emotional suffering that pushed me to do something different. A mental and emotional bottom is getting sick and tired of being sick and tired. I had to hit a bottom with people pleasing the same way that I did with crack cocaine, by getting sick and tired of being sick and tired of doing the same things over and over again. Keep in mind addictions can be behaviors—not just substances. Addiction is such a cunning enemy of life because it zaps all of the energy of self-sufficiency. That's why some things are better not tried. I won't play the lotto or gamble because, if I win *once*, I'm off to the races trying to win all the time. I understand how addictive my personality is so I refuse to try stuff to keep from adding another problem to my life of addiction. Addiction is an outside fix for an inside solution and it cannot work for two reasons.

The first is that we can't grow through our problems because we use something from the outside to fix the inside. When we don't grow internally through our problems and situations, we never learn how to build character and trust ourselves. The situations I go through reveal me to myself so that I might know where I stand in life mentally and emotionally. Life is not set up for us to win or lose, but to grow. It's in growing that we win. If we don't grow we can't win and be happy. If we're not happy, we'll look for something to make us happy and addiction becomes our lot in life.

The next reason addiction doesn't work is that it is only temporary. Whatever our addiction is, we do it to feel good for the moment. Once it's over, the pain comes back. We become addicted to trying to erase the pain permanently...*by any means necessary*.

There was a time in my life when I believed I could not function without something in me to make me feel better. I was always trying to change my mood. My main addiction was trying to feel good all the time because I hated to feel bad. As a child, I started reaching outside of myself for something to make me feel good. Much of the time, it was a means of mental and emotional survival. This continued into my adult life. I would smoke marijuana every chance I got – first thing in the morning, at lunchtime, and all night. What I was trying to do was to make my "good" mood last forever because I wanted to stay mentally detached from the world for as long as I could. It was like a dog chasing his tail, never realizing that the tail can't be caught. That's what trying to stay high all the time was like – it could not be done. I don't know why it is called "getting high" when in actuality it takes us lower.

Addictions are an attempt to escape reality and not deal with the real problems inside of us. We are all addicted to feeling good, no matter how we go about doing it.

My very first addiction was *people-pleasing*. Not knowing anything about addiction it was a survival tool to help me get through a mentally painful childhood. As a child, people-pleasing was a help. As an adult, it became a hindrance and an addiction that caused me more problems than it was worth. People-pleasing was not the problem but the symptom – never feeling worthy or good enough was the problem. At the core of my being, I harbored negative feelings and believed I was never good enough. I covered up those negative feelings by pleasing others, hoping it would make me feel good about myself. I would always give away a better deal than I would keep for myself. People watched me *short-change* myself and got what they wanted. This is the stuff that causes addiction. Addiction happens because of the unwanted negative feelings inside when we try to live outside of ourselves. Our actions rebel against our thoughts.

The thing about addiction that we should remember is: the things we use to avoid our problems will become new problems because of dependency and abuse. I've never met a person with only one addiction.

Let's take a look at my chain of addictions and maybe you will see how yours connect.

My very first *addiction* was *people-pleasing*. Because it stopped working to mask the emotional pain, I needed something new to hide behind. So, I added *sex* to the mix. The sex worked for a while to relieve the negative energy caused by people-pleasing. Now, it's people-pleasing and sex controlling my life. At a point, both addictions stopped working to hide my negative emotions. But I did not stop doing them; I looked for something new to add to the pot. Here, I picked up *alcohol* and I thought I found a savior. At this point, it's people-pleasing, sex, and alcohol and they still leave me wanting.

Stay with me because I'm painting a picture of my life in the hope it will make you look at yours too.

So, I add *marijuana* and I'm off to the races. I believe I have the right combination to live the rest of my life; however, the marijuana got boring and made me eat and sleep. One day, because of my need to escape and my openness to try anything once, I'm introduced to *crack cocaine*...we all know the end of this story. I lost everything...including my mind.

The reason we have so many addictions in our lives is that we *add on* to our problems but *never add up* the problems. Until we get to the exact nature of the problems and pull them up by the roots, the problems will always grow somewhere else in our lives. We never stop anything; rather, we continue to add on until our lives become a continuing cycle of struggling from one addiction to another. Switching addictions is like switching seats on the Titanic. We believe that, if we move where there is no water, we will survive; however, we fail to realize that the whole boat is sinking. The same is true with our lives. We're sinking but hope to survive by switching addictions. It's important to understand that freedom in one area of our lives doesn't necessarily mean freedom in another. Just because we stop one addition, it does not free us from all of the others. There has to be *a bottom* in each area before we become willing to do something.

When I stopped smoking cigarettes it didn't stop me from shopping to my emotions or overeating. Each addiction had to be dealt with directly. My life shows the importance of getting to the root of the problem. I did not want to spend the rest of my life working on the symptoms. Symptoms are always the effect not the cause. I could not change my life because I was working on symptoms and what I discovered was that I had to work on those feelings I stuffed as a child that caused me negative energy. This was the most painful part of addiction – discovering *why* I was doing those things so I would stop killing myself.

Everything goes back to the beginning. We were not born addicts…we became addicts. Whether we want to admit it or not, we are all addicts because we are *creatures of habit* and *habits are addictions*.

Too much of anything is not good if we get out of balance with it.

I'm the kind of person who can take something good and make it bad by doing too much of it. I remember reading my Bible so much that I became so heavenly bound I was no earthly good. Folks began to call me "Reverend" because every time they saw me I was giving them a sermon. I would go out to try to "save the world," not realizing that the world doesn't want to be saved. Then one day on my "save the world" tour, I noticed that the guys standing in front of the 7-11 convenience store began walking away when they saw me coming. I took something good and turned it into bad because I was out of balance with it and myself. Balance is the key to life. Being out of balance will cause pain even if it's doing something good.

To break positive addictions that we are out of balance with and negative ones, we must get to know ourselves. Awareness is the key to breaking addiction. Without awareness, we cannot possibly know why we do what we do or even when we are doing it. Self-awareness is the ability to mentally notice ourselves. Because we have conditioned responses to everything, it's important to be aware of how we respond to life and how we handle stress. For example, if we use food when we're stressed, when stress shows up food will play across the screen of our minds. If we use sex when we're bored, sex will run through our minds as an alternative to the boredom. Many people don't realize that boredom is pain to our minds and it looks for ways to be released. We cause ourselves a lot of pain trying not to be bored. If running from our problems is how we deal with them, when the hard challenges come we string up our mental running shoes and look for ways to escape. It is important to understand how we cope with the stress in our lives and find healthier ways to cope. Addiction is a way of coping that never solves the problem but prolongs the misery. We can't take something bad out of our lives without putting something good in its place. Whatever it was that we stopped became a way of life that took up an amount of time that needs to be filled. If we do not fill that void, we will return to what we do best and that will destroy us. A void is created in our lives when we stop acting out on an addiction. Every void must be filled or the old ways return. When those old habits return, they come back stronger than before. To live wrong when we know how to live right doesn't work anymore because we cannot claim ignorance as an excuse.

I know people-pleasing is an addiction of mine. When I fall into it, I know immediately because of the uncomfortable feelings I get in my gut. That's how change begins – wanting to do something about those uncomfortable feelings.

Here are the *C's* to changing our lives. The first "C" is to *confront*. We must confront our past and present situations so that we might live at last. Confrontation is mentally healthy. If we do not confront those situations, the result will be mental illness or trying to release those negative feelings through addiction.

I hated confrontations, so I let people walk all over my emotions. Then, I would get into my truck and begin to talk to myself about what I should have said. It took me more than two years to tell my next-door neighbor to buy himself a lawnmower because he was using and abusing mine. When I know that I have to confront someone I will practice in the mirror what I will say but, when it's time to say it, I freeze. Today, I am confronting and it's a struggle. However, I realize that I *must* continue working in this area if I want to stop being addicted to everything looking for relief.

The next *C* is *confession*. Telling someone else "the *whole* story" with no holds barred is the way to free the mind from the prison of the past. Our minds stay locked in the past by bringing the experiences of the past into the present through our thoughts. Once the whole story is told, it's not a secret anymore and we can be set free.

The third *C* is *consistency*. We must work on the consistency in applying new information to our minds while confessing the old. In time, our belief system will change. It is *changing what we believe* that will change our lives.

The last *C* is for *continuous*. The process of change *must be* continuous in order to produce the desired result and to keep us from reverting back to old ways of thinking or decision-making. In conclusion let me leave you with this joke.

There's a joke about a guy who wanted to buy a brain so he went to a place where they sold brains. The salesman had three brains left for sale and the guy inquired how much for each one. The first brain was that of a scientist – the salesman wanted $2 million for it. The next brain was that of a doctor and the salesman wanted $1 million for it. The last brain was that of an addict and the salesman wanted $10 million for it. The guy was floored by the price of the addict's brain and asked why so much as compared to the others. The salesman replied that the brain of the addict was almost new. It's never been used.

Remember, addiction is the same hook…just different bait. Many of us work on the bait and forget that the problem is the hook. Do not be confused about which one to work on. The work must be done on the hook, which is the behavior or emotion.

8

SEX OR SIN

I BELIEVE IT'S A SIN *not to understand sex* because it is a part of who we are. Sex is not bad but the information we get is usually lacking in some way. Many parents are reluctant to talk openly with their children about sex, so the children learn from their peers who are also misinformed. It is important to get an understanding of sex if we want to be whole. We do not want to fall victim to emotional wars fought inside of ourselves.

Sex has gotten such a bad rap because of all the things for which it is used. Sex sells cars, music, and houses; it gets jobs and loses jobs; it determines what television shows we watch. Sex can be a source of joy or it can be a source of pain. Since the beginning of time people have destroyed lives and livelihoods because of sex. It can become a stumbling block to higher living.

One thing about sex I am sure of: *when introduced into our lives too early* – whether through molestation, incest, or curiosity – *it can mess us up for the rest of our lives*. However, there is relief from the prison of your mind *if* you have the capacity to be honest about how it was introduced. Those of us who are emotional prisoners must deal with this part of our lives immediately, primarily because our introduction to sex felt more like *sin*.

Sex is one of those things that affects our bodies and disturbs our souls. Of all the things that caused me pain, sex did the most damage mentally and emotionally. Sex was introduced to me through subliminal messages, never through actual teachings. Listening to my mother have sex through paper thin walls when she thought I was asleep stirred up a desire in me at an early age. I wanted to experience that. I tried having sex with the girls with whom I played house with in the backyard. I ended up having sex with an older relative at the age of 8. I did not wake up one day and decide to be a sex addict. It was the way things progressed and, because no one felt comfortable talking about it, my curiosity and experiences led me to become *trapped* by ignorance. I was so ignorant that I thought the vagina was on top of the stomach. No one spoke honestly to me about the consequences of *not knowing* so I continued to act as if I knew. As a result, I went into the abuse stage very early in my life because of the way sex made me feel. I wanted to feel that way all the time.

Keep in mind the three phases of addiction—use, abuse, and bottom. Because I was not properly educated about sex, I skipped the *use* phase. I went directly to abuse and then bottom. It was what I used to avoid the emotional problems on the inside. I used sex the same way I used crack cocaine – as an emotional outlet to release pent-up negative emotional energy. The bottom came about 20 years later as the abuse caused me more problems than it solved so I went into therapy. Talking honestly to the therapist allowed me to understand and take control of this addiction. The next step was to continue going to therapy and telling the truth about myself that I had originally planned to take to my grave. This experience taught me that sex was not bad; it becomes bad because of misinformation that causes us to abuse it.

There must be total exposure of our sexual past if we want the healing process to begin. Exposure is important because sickness grows in secret and dies in the light of honesty. It will be very uncomfortable in the beginning, but feel the fear and do it anyway. We cannot begin to heal until we begin to tell the truth about our hidden self – the person that only *we* know. We don't have to write a book or tell the world but we have to tell at least one person who we really are, not who we want folks to think we are. There are a lot of people today going through life hurting and broken because of sexual abuse and misuse. If we do not work to heal ourselves, our children will continue to suffer the consequences.

Sex is God's greatest expression of love between a man and a woman; however, too many of us start our lives with sexual scars and wounds from our childhood. So, it was important to start at the beginning and recall *how* sex was introduced into our lives.

When I look back, I noted that I had sick behavior about sex long before I became an adult. Understanding and awareness helped me see that. It was only through conscious awareness that I was able to change my behavior. The only time to make a decision is in an awakened or conscious state. I learned to change my life with my conscious mind.

Learning to make good choices moment by moment is how I changed my life. Through an honest exchange with my therapist, I learned that I did not have to choose for the entire day – just for the moment. If I made a bad choice at a point during the day, I needed to accept that and have the willingness and courage to make the next right choice. Asking for what I needed sexually from my relationship was crucial. In my relationships, I never asked for what I wanted. I settled for less and acted out through addiction. Either we meet our needs in a healthy way or we meet them in an unhealthy way. Either way, our needs will be met.

Too many relationships are held together by everything but love. Children are usually the glue that holds us together. Having children should not be the cause of sex; rather, it should be the result of love expressed through sex. Sex without love is painful and empty. A sex addict feels the pain and emptiness but because of habit will continue to try to make it work. We must begin to give ourselves the love we need in order to change for the better.

We need to stop talking about the birds and the bees and start talking about the vagina and penis. The birds and the bees don't get young girls pregnant; a young man full of energy does. It's not the birds and the bees passing sexually transmitted diseases; ignorance and sexual addiction are the causes. When we don't inform our children about sex because it feels uncomfortable to us, we set them up for a fall. We must tell them that it's God-given and the purpose is to create other human beings in our own image. Our children must know the consequences of having sex for fun. The need to feel good should not become more important than dying. It's a shame to live with something that's a part of that which we are and yet have no understanding of how to use it correctly.

As a result of being out of control sexually I've caught many sexually transmitted diseases including one I can't get rid of – Herpes. I haven't been told I have HIV but if I were I would not like it but would accept the fact because of all the places I've put myself unprotected trying to feel good. This was the consequence of my *not knowing*.

Another problem permeating this society is how sex is used as a leveraging tool. Leveraging means to control a lot of something with a little. An example of leveraging is buying a $100,000 house with only $500 dollars down—you control a lot with a little. The same is true with sex. We leverage our lives with sex. It is used by the wife as punishment or reward depending on what her husband does. The boss uses the job to have sex with the employee. The husband uses leaving or violence to bring his wife into submission. Sex is part of our lives, not all of it.

Stop and think for a moment about how much of our world is controlled by sex in one way or another. Look at how much suffering is the result of not understanding the ramifications of our instincts in overdrive. HIV is not decreasing itsSex or sin is a matter of understanding. It's sex when we understand the purpose. It becomes sin because of ignorance.

PART TWO

Solutions

9

THE BLAME GAME

THE FIRST STEP TO CHANGING OUR LIVES is to accept responsibility for where we are in life at this very moment. We could not choose our parents, our siblings, or where we grew up, but we do have the choice of how we live our lives today. It is critical that we accept things the way they are right now and *not blame* anyone or anything, so that we can move forward with the healing of our minds and souls.

All work is mental. Every action, interaction, and reaction starts in the mind. It's not our fault how we started life but it is our responsibility how we finish. Blame is a weak excuse used for a poor life that is not going anywhere.

We use blame to be irresponsible; it keeps us stuck looking to the external and not the internal for the answers to our lives. The definition for blame is to hold someone or something at fault, to *absolve* responsibility. When we blame we are saying, in essence, it's someone else's fault for our conditions and it's *their job* to fix us.

Nobody in the world can say "I quit" about my life but me. No one can start living for me and no one can quit living for me. Some may get in my way and delay me but no one can deny me of the things that are for me if I'm willing to work for them.

It is true that the people close to me as a child contributed to my mental and emotional illness; however, it is a waste of time to believe that they will help to make me well. They can't because they have yet to make the choice to work on themselves because they are still mentally and emotionally sick. My parents, relatives, and others who "nurtured" and taught me have a story because they were children too. Until something or someone makes them look at their lives, denial and ignorance will keep them sick. The biggest lesson I learned was if I wanted the people in my life to change for the better, I needed to make some positive changes in my life.

How many times have you tried to give an honest opinion to your family and friends and they reject or deny it? It is a total waste of time to work on someone else's life. Keep the focus on yourself so that you might break the cycle.

Blame must be dealt with before the work can begin because it gets in the way of healing. Until we take full responsibility for making our lives better, we cannot grow. When we change for the better, the people in our lives have to change for the better because *we tend to attract who we are*. When we begin to work on ourselves and put the new information into action, we will begin to remove those negative forces out of our lives or they will leave on their own.

In the Garden of Eden, Adam blamed Eve, Eve blamed the snake, and God put them all out. Not even God allows blame as an excuse for making bad decisions. People blame the devil but fail to realize that they still have to be responsible and held accountable for their choices.

Blame and forgiveness are at the opposite ends of the same spectrum. If you drew a line and put blame on one end and forgiveness on the other, where would *you* be on the line? Well, that depends on where your life is headed at this moment.

When my life wasn't going anywhere, I was either close to, or at, the blame end of the spectrum. Now that my life is going somewhere...and I've taken *full responsibility* to make my life better...I'm close to, or at, the forgiveness end of the spectrum. In order for my life to move forward, I had to overcome a lot of mental and emotional barriers. When I climbed over those hurdles, I could see the sickness in others. And that having compassion was a natural state of mind once the work was done.

Forgiveness, coupled with the understanding of self, leads to the healing of the mind that allows us the freedom to understand others'. We must stop blaming and start healing by taking control of our own lives and directing our lives where we want it to go. To accomplish this, we must be willing to make the hard decisions and accept the consequences of those decisions.

We all have personal challenges to overcome, so why "point the finger" or place blame?

10

LIVE BY CHOICE
OR CHANCE

OUR PRIMARY JOB ON EARTH is that we are decision-makers—nothing more or less. We are the only creation that God created that has the ability to make decisions. We make decisions that conform to what we believe. Until we change what we believe we can't change the decisions we make. Learning and growing from the consequences of our choices will make us better decision-makers.

To live by choice means we are *proactive* not reactive. Proactive means *"before actions"* or *preventative* measures. If I take action before it is needed, my life will improve tremendously. The most challenging time to work on ourselves is when things are going good. To be proactive means to work on ourselves consistently, even when "the storm is calm" and "the winds are still."

When we live our lives by chance, it's like playing the lotto. We randomly select the numbers and there is the *possibility* we might win. We do the same thing with our lives when we live by chance, randomly making decision and hoping *this time* we will get lucky. Maybe we will win the jackpot (a better life). A life lived by chance is one of indecisiveness and confusion, often followed by pain. When living by chance, we only work on ourselves when things go badly; that is, if we do it at all. By then it will be too late because, at this point, we're merely looking for relief. We haven't planned; we haven't taken any preventative action; therefore, we do *random* "activity" or take sporadic action, hoping for the "quick fix." As soon as things calm down in our lives, we stop working on ourselves. Ultimately, the consequences of our indecisiveness and confusion cause the pain to return. As time passes, we become locked into a certain way of thinking that is controlled by complacency, complaining, unreliability, and stagnation.

People of chance don't like to make decisions. Not to make a decision means we had to make a decision *not to* make one, so we still made a decision. Because many of us try not to make bad decisions, we end up stuck in indecisiveness. To be indecisive is akin to spinning our wheels in the mud, burning a lot of energy, but not going anywhere.

My life is better today because I make better decisions. I had to *learn how* to do that. The first thing I did was to get better information in my head so I could make an *informed* decision. Next, I had to have the courage *to act* on the new information. Without the courage to take action, the information merely becomes useless words.

We can read all the positive and motivational books in the world but, without applying the knowledge to our daily lives, all of the reading is in vain. We can begin by not being concerned about what others may think or say, move forward with our decisions, and assume responsibility for those decisions.

Growth work is reading the books, listening to motivational tapes, surrounding ourselves with positive people, and honestly talking about ourselves when things are going good or bad, so that we are better prepared to handle life situations because of our *proactive* mental growth. We must learn to prepare for war in a time of peace...we must stop waiting until it rains to buy an umbrella. We must stop waiting until there is a crisis in our lives or we hurt as a result of indecision to begin to do the work on ourselves.

A person living by choice is *driven*. A *driven* person makes things happen – he/she *initiates* action and expects a positive result. A person living by chance is *pushed*. The *pushed* person waits for things to happen – he/she *reacts* irresponsibly.

There are three types of people in this world: those who make things happen; those who wait for things to happen; and those who don't know what's happening. A driven person learns to take things in stride knowing that things happen *for them* not to them. They set goals and are harder on themselves so their lives will be easier. They do not *kick* themselves when they make mistakes; rather, they "stay on top" of their life issues; they are "sure-footed" in their decision making; and they do not make excuses. Driven people go to the library because they believe self-education is far more important than entertaining themselves. Driven people pay their bills on time and, sometimes, ahead of time to stay ahead of the game. Driven people accept help from others but their actions are not based on what someone else may do for them – if the help comes...fine; if not...that's fine too.

Now on the other hand, we have the *pushed* people. Those folks always need someone to hold their hands so they won't fall and get hurt. If they fall, they make it your job to pick them up, by using guilt and self-pity. A pushed person needs someone to stay on top of them all the time. They need constant reminding to do the things that need to be done. They are forever pointing fingers, placing blame, and making excuses for not changing their lives, while being a burden to other people who are trying to live. You have to double check them to see if they paid the bills on time; call their jobs to see if they showed up for work; or buy books that they still don't read. The next time you go out into the world, start listening and you will hear the pushed people. They are loud and complaining about their situations and everything else; yet, they are content in doing nothing to resolve anything in their lives.

Many of us came out of families that were of the "pushed" variety, relying on God to drop out of the sky, make all of our decisions, and work out the consequences. *Newsflash*...it doesn't work that way! We make the decisions and God creates our decisions in the physical world.

When I ride through the streets of Washington, D.C., I see people sleeping on the ground or at the bus stops. I don't say, "There's a poor person"; rather, I say there's a poor decision-maker. I know this to be a fact because I slept on those same streets. Even at my lowest point, *I still had to make a decision* to change my life. God didn't come down, grab me by the hand, and *walk* me to a drug treatment facility. I had to make the decision to get up and get some help, and God created my decision in the physical world.

We are never victims in this life as long as we understand that we are decision-makers. Until we make a different decision, our results will be the same. To be indecisive means we are double-minded and to be double-minded is to be unstable. *The only power we have is the power of choice.* Giving up our right to choose is giving up our right to live. When we make decisions based on what others think, our lives begin to look like their beliefs. To consciously make a decision to do nothing to improve our lives means that, subconsciously, we made the decision to stay the same—*it is by choice.* We can't change our lives with our subconscious mind because the ability to choose is a part of our conscious mind. We must *consciously choose* to change our lives.

There's a guy in my neighborhood that does one thing every day – he begs for change. He doesn't understand that the real change is mental. I made the decision to stop giving him money because he has to make a decision every day to get up from wherever he is to come stand in front of the store and beg for change. Until he decides to do something different, nothing in his life will change for the better.

We are neither winners nor losers; rather, we are chooser. Our choices will determine which one we will become. Inside each and every one of us lives a winner and a loser; so winning or losing is a matter of choice. We are all self-made at the level of choice, no matter how we were raised. This is a spiritual law of life that cannot be changed. It doesn't make sense to fight the law by blaming other people but work with the law through understanding it is our *choice*. Only through acquiring new information and acting on it can we make the law work for us and not against us.

We must make the choice to upgrade our mental software by seeking new information about the world we live in and our spirituality; then decide how we fit into the world. The choice to feed our minds must be made every-day until the new information becomes habit – the habit of positive thinking. We cannot do anything without first making a decision to do it. Even something seemingly trivial, like going to the bathroom now or holding it until later, involves choice.

To whom much is given, much is required. We have been given the ability to choose and that means we have the gift of creativity. The ability to create is the greatest expression of God's power in us. Of everything God created, he gave only humankind the ability to choose. All other life forms are driven by instinct. More is required of us than to merely say "we're blessed" because we woke up this morning. Dogs and cats woke up too. Waking up is not our choice, *it's what we do after we get up* that's our choice. We are creating every moment of our lives, whether we know it or not, by the choices we make.

Prayer without action teaches us how to suffer better. It's only through prayer, self-improvement, and making better decisions that our lives will change. God does not solve our problems; rather, God uses us to solve the problems we created.

When we live by chance we pray a lot but do very little to change our lives. We make bad decisions about our health so our bodies break down and we go broke trying to fix it. We won't make the decision to exercise but continue to complain about being overweight and out of shape. People make the decision to smoke cigarettes but they don't want cancer. There is an endless list of things that we want but deny them with the choices we make. The power of choice that was given to us for freedom has meant bondage for many.

So how do we stop living by chance and start living by choice?

First, we must become readers. Readers are leaders and leaders are readers. I'm a firm believer that the person who *does not* read isn't any better off than the person who *cannot* read. Either way, there is no new information taken in. Without new information, there cannot be a new choice.

Also, we need to remove two words from our lives. Those words are *easy* and *fair*. Life is not easy and it will never be fair. We have a tendency to confuse the word easy with simple: life is very simple but it's not easy to keep it simple. The truths inherent in life are always simple so that everyone can grasp them but, because of bad information, we miss the easy lessons. Also, if life were fair, there would be no need for police, judges, lawyers, referees, and umpires. People are just not fair all of the time.

In order to live by choice, we must get M.A.D.D. at life. The "M" is for motivation. The "A" is for appreciation. The first "D" is for dedication. The Last "D" is for discipline. We must start motivating ourselves to do better. We live in a de-motivating world where folks always remind us of our short falls. We must become self-starters who can move forward on their own. For example, if we got mugged we should not expect the mugger to come back and pick us up...we must make the decision to pick up ourselves and go on. The same is true about life: when the unpredictability mugs us, let's get up mentally and move forward with the business of living. Everything that has been hard has not necessarily been worth it; however, everything that's worth it has been hard.

Self-starters don't look for easy or fair but have a desire to be the best they can be and are willing to pay the price. Self-starters program their minds to win through the use of self-improvement books, motivational tapes, and seminars on whatever is needed in their lives to give them the mental advantage.

Next we must learn to appreciate life and all the beauty it displays; the wonder of how everything follows a plan that was set in place before time. There must be appreciation for each other, and that we still have a chance to get things right between us before it's too late. We need to understand that we can die at every next moment so we need to stop taking life for granted. Appreciation is about living life to its fullest potential, while at the same time adding new knowledge to grow to higher highs. It's looking back to see where you came from and appreciating where you are, because it could have gone the other way.

I appreciate the hard road I traveled to get to where I am because I would not be the person I am today. I appreciate the experience of smoking crack cocaine and losing my mind. Losing everything helped me find what I was looking for…it helped me find myself.

Third, we need to work on our dedication… making a commitment to something and setting a course of action to achieve whatever the goal. We must be dedicated to ourselves when it comes to changing our lives. Keeping our word to ourselves should be the number one priority; we must keep integrity with ourselves. We must make a commitment to change our lives and stick to that commitment. We spend too much time making commitments to help other people change their lives while letting our own lives go down the drain. The first commitment must be to us. All else is people pleasing. Without a firm commitment, change will be hard because we won't stick and stay when things get tough. To be committed means that we push ourselves when our emotions try to trap us. The uncommitted person lives and acts on feelings, which is an emotional trap. Making the commitment to change means we watch what we eat when we set the goal to lose weight. Commitment will make us stick to our budget when we are working to get out of debt. Our lives don't get better until we make the commitment to make it better.

Last, but certainly not least, is discipline. Discipline is training expected to produce a specific skill, behavior, or character and controlled behavior resulting from such training. Disciplined means we train our minds to obey us. When we obey our minds we act impulsively on the thoughts that enter it – we react based on how we feel at that moment. When we do what's right, regardless of what may be going through our minds and how we may feel at a given moment, our mind is obeying us. Disciplined mental training is the application of powerful information to the mind to produce a specific behavior or character. Now, put the word *self* in front of discipline and work accordingly.

Self-discipline is the foundation of freedom and the brother of change. Any areas in my life where I don't have self-discipline, I am a prisoner to that area. Self-discipline is *the catalyst* to change. Without it, all work is sporadic. Self-discipline creates consistency and consistency produces change.

Choose to make the decision to make the commitment to change your life for the better.

Here's a story of the process of change by choice:

I walk down the street. I fall in a hole. It's not my fault and it takes me a long time to get out.

The next day I walk down the same street, fall into the same hole. It's still not my fault but it takes me even longer to get out.

The next day I walk down the same street and fall into the same hole. *It is my fault* and I get out immediately.

The next day I walk down the same street. I see the hole and I go around it.

The next day, I go down another street.

11

TALK LIFE NOT DEATH

MANY OF US SPEAK DEATH and defeat into our lives by the words we use daily. There is power in the tongue. People who do not control their tongues will find it hard to change their belief system.

The reason the mouth must be controlled is because our belief system responds to what it hears the most. If we constantly talk negatively, then our belief system will respond by turning that information into the truth. As time passes, our lives will look like what we've been saying all the time. I hear people say all the time, "they're hanging in there," or, "they're trying to make it." It's a shame to see the results of that kind of talk.

It's a down right disgrace to God to reduce life to hanging, and holding on, when we should be creating. Out of everything God created, we are the only ones with the ability to use words, everything else responds to words. We create through the use of words and because no one truly takes this seriously we talk ourselves into dying and defeat. Human beings create through the use of words and animals are trained to respond as a result of words. But when you look out into the world and at your own life you will see that we are taught to respond, not create, by the words used in our childhood.

In the beginning was the word and the word was with God and the word was God. Everything that God created wasn't here already but was spoken into existence by the power inherent in words. So God gave us the same power to speak things into existence through the power of the spoken word and it doesn't matter if it's positive or negative, whatever we speak happens.

Change always starts with new words of power. To change, we must speak the words we would like to become; and if the words coming out of our mouth are negative, then shut up. All words have power but the ones I speak and believe the most have power over my life. I believed that something was wrong with me because of the words others used against me in an attempt to be funny. It wasn't funny to me but I internalized it as the truth, so I spent a great deal of my life feeling inadequate. I had to start using words of love, and forgiveness on myself, in order to heal my mind. Isn't that what affirmations are all about; saying you love yourself when you don't.

This whole world operates off of words, just start to notice how everything, in one-way or another, must be transmitted some how through words. Even people who are blind or deaf must learn how to use words, either through Braille or sign language. The spirit, or God, only responds to words we believe and send out by our thoughts. Thoughts are words that are seen, and not spoken. Listen to the world and you will notice a defeated and pessimist tone dominating the land. To say you're blessed, and your life is full of chaos, then the words that you speak are like sounding brass, loud and empty.

Part of the process of change is using words to push you forward toward your goals. Not the ones that slow the process or stop it all together. Give yourself an advantage by using words that empower you, not make you powerless. The word empower means power from within, and until we learn to use the power from within, our lives will be of no avail. When we use words of power consistently it has a tendency to empower us. I want results out of my life not regrets so I use words of power to strengthen my mind; to push through my emotions. Because I stay on top of the words that come out of my mouth and yours too, people have started to call me names like the motivator or Mr. Kim and at times have gotten mad because I confront them on the words they say. It's not that I'm trying to save the world but guard my mind from negative seeds being planted because it's easy for me to attach my mind to negativity. When I say something to you about the way you're speaking it's to help you to see the power of words and also to protect me if I must be around you a lot. Now if it's in passing most of the time I'll just let it fly over my head but I refuse to be around negative talking people for any length of time. To understand the power of words will help you for the journey ahead which will get easier as you stay committed to watching the words you use the most. This understanding will increase your power over yourself, because it will train the mind to obey you.

To have power we must educate ourselves which is words coming together to make sense about something. The word educate means to provide with knowledge and knowledge is aware-ness and understanding. That means, we must seek new information, which is knowledge derived from study, experience, or instruction. Everyone at some time in their lives should edu-cate themselves about themselves. When we become educated it means we have knowledge and knowledge is said to be power and power is the ability to act effectively. But knowledge is not power until we act on it. We can not act effective-ly if we don't have knowledge of who we are so we can't walk in power. Now we can have knowl-edge in a certain field and act effectively in that field but life is more than just a one- subject course. When I see people using words of anger to control another to try and show real power, I know that's not real power but just a show. Real power is not loud or angry, it's tempered in love and understanding and is seldom heard.

One day I watched a young man bark out com-mands to his dog and the dog obeyed. He took on a sense of pride for the control that he had over the dog by the simple use of words. While I was sitting at the red light pondering the scene, a thought came to me, I wonder if he could control his own life. Just like the dog obeyed, we are all conditioned to obey, even if it's wrong. Words are the tools used to condition everyone, this is a fact, if you know it or not. What is conditioning? It's the process of using words consistently until we get the desired result.

Here's an example of how the conditioning process works. We bought a cat when it was a kitten, and decided on what name we wanted to call her—or condition her to respond to. So we chose Precious, and for the next few months every time we saw the kitten we would call her Precious. Now, the kitten ran up and down the stairs, never responding to the name we chose, it was as if she said "I don't know who they're talking to." But because of consistency, which is the operative word, she responded one day, and came to us when we called her Precious. We sealed the conditioning process by giving her a treat for listening. Now, how hard would it be to change her name? The chances are slim to none that she would respond. If this works on a kitten that can't

use words, how well would it work on an inno-
cent child? That's why as adults we must use
words of power on ourselves to raise up the child
from within. Because this process is long, and
hard, most people would rather just stay the same
and complain.

I was already doomed to failure before I started life, because of all the words of negativity spoken to me as a child. When I realized that I was
born to win, but conditioned to lose, I set out on
a journey of self-discovery, which is the greatest
trip in the world. I've overcome a lot of things in
my life, but none can compare to breaking the
conditioning process of failure. I would have victory working in my life, and find a way to defeat
myself, because deep down inside, I always felt
so unworthy, or undeserving of the good things of
life. Words were used to condition me to lose, so
I must use words to condition myself to win.
Most people are lazy when it comes to reading as
a way of breaking bad thought habits, so don't
follow the group and save your own life.
Remember you're not trying to save the world,
but change your life. Save yourself and leave the
world to its own undoing.

I read myself out of the conditioning process of failure and found my greatness. We all have been endowed with greatness but few will ever be great because of negative words turned into negative beliefs. You don't have to be great to get started but you have to get started to be great. Notice I use the word great instead of good because it takes the same energy to say either but the results are different. If you shoot for the moon and miss at least you'll land amongst the stars. Talk small, believe small, and you live small. Talk big, believe big, and you live big. And remember the words I speak today will be the life I live tomorrow so chose your words with care because your life depends on it. There's a saying that says "Sticks and stones may break my bones but words will never hurt me." They don't hurt because they kill and destroy us.

12

MIND OVER MATTER

THE MIND IS OUR GREATEST ASSET. If we don't learn how to use it properly, nothing else matters.

The definition of the mind is "the consciousness that directs mental and physical behavior." Consciousness is the awareness of our own existence, sensations, thoughts, and environment. So, the mind is being conscious of who we are, what we feel, what we think and where we are. It's the ability to process things going on in us and around us at all times. Many of us learned to live our lives by using our minds unconsciously, so we really don't know who we are and have no idea where we're going. We tend to stay lost because of the zombies we live with who have no clue either. We fit right in and it feels normal, primarily because we don't know any better, so we settle for less and complain about more.

Negative information turned into negative belief makes us reject the constant voice of awareness that tells us we should be doing more than we are doing with our lives. People who do not work to improve themselves and learn to control their minds have thoughts like stray bullets – they are bound to go out and do some harm.

"Be ye transformed by the renewing of your mind." In the spiritual sense, transformed means the container will look the same but the content will be different. When I talk about the mind I am not referring to the brain. The mind and the brain are two very different things. The brain is tangible; the mind is intangible. We cannot see, touch, or feel the mind, but we know it's there. The mind has no physical features but it has awesome spiritual power.

Connected to the brain are the nose, mouth, ears, eyes, and hands; all are information channels that allow us to smell, taste, hear, see, and touch. These five senses allow us to retrieve information from the physical world through the conscious mind and turn it into spiritual information for the mind to act on.

In order to change our lives, we must change what we look at, what we listen to, and what we say. We must use our information channels to control our minds by selecting the information we allow to enter or keep out of it. We select the food we eat and the clothes we wear. We must learn to be equally selective about the information that we allow into our heads. The mind doesn't care if the information is negative or positive it takes what it's being fed and goes about the business of creating the life it has been told to create. If we don't learn to control our minds, we will be controlled by it, acting on impulse – if it feels good, do it...no matter the consequence.

The mind can be controlled but it must be done through the use of powerful, positive information that is applied daily until we achieve the desired result. The results vary, depending upon what we want out of life.

Whether or not we know it, we tell our minds what life we want to live by the information we operate off of. As children, we take in all of the information around us and internalize it as truths. The information fed and internalized as children determines our lives as adults. When we are trapped behind the bars of our thoughts, the bad information translated into negative belief; consequently, turned our minds into jail cells where our souls are serving time. The difference between positive information and negative information is we have to look for positive information; negative information finds us.

In keeping with this, it is crucial to reflect on how we started life because that's where our belief system was created and the mind creates only what we believe. The mind is God's way of giving us the power to subdue and have dominion over the earth. The mind is not the place for thinking; rather, it is a place for mental activity. "Thinking" is an all encompassing word designed to mean "mental activity." Few understand how this activity takes place so we create our own problems and pray to God to fix them.

The activities of the mind are belief, thought, free Will, faith, ego, subconscious, and consciousness – all of which connect us to God.

In the following paragraphs, I will talk about how the mind works and how to use it to produce your greatness. I will begin with the most important part of the mind, which is the only part that can be changed, and that is belief.

Believe It or Not

What are beliefs? Beliefs are the mental acceptance of, or conviction in, the truth or actuality of something. Something believed in that is accepted as truth. Beliefs are information we receive from the world around us and internalize it as truth, whether it is or not. We can believe something that's not true but to us it is true because it is the only information we were given. With this, we become narrow-minded in our views.

Once information is accepted as the truth, it is the truth to whoever is accepting it. Our beliefs are stored in the mind by way of the ego. The ego is our spiritual heart where everything springs forth into existence. When we talk about what's in a person's heart, we're not talking about the physical, tangible heart that pumps blood. We are talking about the spiritual heart, which is in our mind and contains everything we believe.

We were not born with a belief system; we developed it over time through physical experience. Along with the belief system, we developed an ego. The ego is simply memory of past physical experience. Because our belief system is created, it can be recreated by selecting new information. Feeding our minds with the new information allows us to push out the old ideas that have become mental and emotional traps.

Our belief system is fully developed by the time we reach age 7 and subsequently becomes a way of life. Our belief system was developed through repetition. As children, we were constantly fed the same information. The difference now is that we have to assume responsibility for the information that goes into our minds where as children, we did not. Keep in mind that beliefs are information that has been internalized as truth, even if it is not. Without new information, we cannot form new beliefs. If we want to change our lives, the only thing that needs to be changed is our belief system.

The word "system" means a group of interrelated, interacting, or interdependent constituents forming a complex whole. Our belief system is a group of interrelated or interacting beliefs about everything we've experienced that makes up a complex whole called life. The point is that we have a lot of beliefs and changing one does not necessarily change the other.

The following is a true story of the importance of changing one's belief system:

There is a guy in my neighborhood who's has been homeless for at least 10 years. Every once in a while someone comes by to pick him up. They take him someplace where he can shower, shave, eat, and get a change of clothes. When he's brought back to our neighborhood, he looks like a different person. He then goes back to the same bus stop, plops in the same spot, and, in time, his outside begins to look like his insides again.

Why is it that "cleaning him up" did not work? Because the only thing that changed about the homeless man was his outward appearance. His belief about himself stayed the same. Therefore, the "good Samaritan" work was only temporary; it was just a mental break from the madness in the homeless man's mind.

Our beliefs become things in the physical world through our thoughts, which is the next part of the mind that needs to be understood.

Thoughts Are Alive

I constantly hear people say they need to change their thinking. The problem is that they do not know what part of their thinking needs to be changed? Many think that it is their thoughts that need changing so they waste time working on something over which they have no control.

We must understand that our thoughts are living, breathing, self-contained entities. No one can start or stop thoughts from coming into their minds; thoughts move on their own energy…it's as if they have a mind of their own.

Thoughts are the connection between what we believe and what God creates in our lives. God doesn't create based on what's right or wrong, he creates based on what we believe and send out by thoughts.

Look at the world and notice how everyone is living their beliefs – from the businessman to the drunk. The physical world consists of beliefs transmitted through thoughts that have become things. Things that are here today were not always here; they came from someone's belief, sent out as a thought, and transformed into a thing. The computer, airplane, car, and microwave are but a few of the thoughts that became things.

Inside of every thought is how something feels, tastes, smells, or sounds. All of the sensations are inherent in the thought. We choose to go places before we leave the house by experiencing the place in our minds through our thoughts before we make a definite choice. There is always a thought before an action, and our lives always follow our thoughts. Thoughts are the interface or connection between our personal mind and the non-personal mind of God.

Our personal mind is what we use to be creative on the earth to manifest our purpose. Without a personal mind, we could not be creative. The non-personal mind of God is the intelligence that's behind everything. It doesn't cater to anyone; rather, it is for use by everyone. Everything lives inside of the non-personal mind of the Spirit because nothing exists outside of God. Man could travel to the ends of the earth and still not be able to get outside of the mind of God. So, if everything is inside of the mind of God, than world is alive with energy and information. That's the message conveyed here – that the world is alive and teeming with energy.

We don't live in a physical world. We live in a spiritual world that has created physical things. Think about it. Why does the television or radio work with just an antenna on top? How are we able to page someone in another state, in a matter of seconds, through satellites in outer space, thousands of miles away? How is it that our cell phones allow us to drive and walk without dropping the call...What gets the information from the cell phone to the cell tower? There is nothing we can see between us and the sky to make that call happen. Man believes that he discovered wireless communication but God has always communicated with us through wireless means by way of thoughts. Thoughts are the wireless way we communicate with God and God with us. The mind receives and transmits thoughts. Remember a time when you thought about someone and a few days later they showed up. Your response was, "I was just thinking about you." We are co-creators with God through our minds. Our challenge has been that we're always at the wrong end of the transaction because we were never taught how thoughts work.

We choose negative thoughts because of negative beliefs and send them out to God by faith to be created in our physical reality. Once we get the negative results, we pray to God to change them. Our place in the creation process with God should be at the beginning not the end, where we choose positive thoughts because of positive beliefs and send them out by faith for processing by God. God takes the thoughts received by faith and creates them in our physical world. It is imperative to understand this concept, if we want to change our lives because God just is and there is no right or wrong in God. If this were not true, why is there so much suffering going on, especially with churchgoers? The reason is God doesn't break his laws of creation because we decide to give him praise. The process of how things are created is through the thoughts of mankind. We cannot praise ourselves into a new way of thinking; we must think ourselves into a new way of living. See how beliefs and thoughts are connected in and through our minds?

Let's look at the cell phone example again. In the air is an invisible energy called carrier waves. A carrier wave carries information from one point to another. Information from the carrier waves is transmitted to the antenna and back to the phone. This same kind of energy is used to carry our thoughts from our minds to God, and for God to send ideas and answers back to us. We say things like, "you know a thought came to me from out of the blue" or, "a thought popped into my head." Learning to control this process is how we create the life we want to live. Our beliefs are put on the carrier wave of thoughts by faith, and sent to God for creating. Be mindful that God just creates by manifesting what we believe and it doesn't make a difference whether it is right or wrong, good or bad. The only way to control this process is to change what we believe. Everything is controlled by what we believe.

In the computer, there is a hard drive where all the information is stored to run the programs. Well, our beliefs are stored on the hard drive in the mind to run a program called life. Everyone has this program and there are no exceptions.

We are under the illusion that we think thoughts. To think thoughts means we can create thoughts. We don't create thoughts but we observe them coming and going in and out of our minds. Thoughts come to us as a result of what we believe and have experienced in life. We do not attract thoughts of things we do not believe or have not experienced.

I have smoked crack cocaine but I've never shot heroin so I don't attract thoughts of shooting heroin; I attract thoughts of smoking crack cocaine. When the thought of smoking crack cocaine comes into my mind, it is so powerful that I physically react to it. I get nervous and my stomach starts to flip. Remember, thoughts are alive and have the sensations of the experience. The reason my stomach flips and I get nervous is because of the energy in the thoughts that causes me to have the experience in my mind.

Because there is no understanding of the energy in thoughts, man blamed the devil. The devil is man's way of explaining the power inherent in thoughts that feel like an attack on his mind. Powerful thoughts feel like an attack and, depending on the degree of negativity of the thought will determine how much mental fighting we must endure. Also, all of the addictions we have in our lives will attract the thoughts of those addictions, especially when we are trying to stop. Temptation is simply the thought of something we don't want to do anymore. To change the thoughts we attract, we must change the magnet that attracts them. Beliefs attract thoughts like a magnet attracts iron.

Using "will power" only lasts for a while. We can only will ourselves to do right for a moment and, sooner or later, the real "us" takes over. We are what we believe we are.

Here's where the reap and sow concept must be understood. We are taught, "You reap what you sow." It's true but we are too far up the road on this concept. Let's go back to the beginning of the creation process where we sow our beliefs through thoughts by faith and reap them as a thing in the physical world. We do reap what we sow but the sowing is mental, not physical. This is a powerful insight that can change the world by changing each person into a creative force for good.

There is nothing we do without the thought to do it first. A thought always happens before action. We need to stop trying to pray ourselves out of something we thought ourselves into. By changing what we believe, we can choose the right thoughts and God can create the right results.

Now let's deal with the part of the mind that connects our beliefs to thoughts, which is faith.

Faith

Everything is done by faith. As a child, I heard the word "faith" used many times but no one explained what it meant. The dictionary definition of Faith is "confident belief in the truth, value, or trustworthiness of a person, idea, or thing." It is belief not based on logical proof or material evidence. Here's a workable, useable everyday understanding of Faith. Faith is focusing on a thought with your belief until it manifests in your physical world, while at the same time rejecting any other thoughts that come up against that which you want to have in your life. Notice I said "Any other thoughts that come up

143

against that which you want to have in your life," because everything outside of us must first become a thought before the mind can act.

We can't stop the defeating thoughts from coming but we have a choice to either let them through and dwell on them, or to dismiss them completely. It's the dwelling or focusing of our minds on thoughts that makes them become real in our reality. So, Faith is mentally focusing on thoughts based on what we believe until they become a physical reality.

When we don't understand how to use faith, we tend to focus on the negative thoughts. The reason we fail at using faith is we think it can be used when we choose to use it. Faith is a working part of the mind, and is always in operation. We tell each other, "Where is your faith" or "have a little faith; it's going to be all right," as if it's something that can be grabbed at will. Because faith is the focusing of the mind on thoughts, it is always in use.

Faith is a process of the mind that is not controlled by anyone but must be directed by everyone to the thoughts of the things we want in our lives. Negative faith, or focusing on the negative, becomes doubt, worry, non-belief, and destruction. Positive faith, or focusing on the positive, is called creativity.

There is another part to faith that is just as important as the rest. It is relaxing the mind in the present moment while the manifestation of what we want is taking place. Faith is a way of being that shows up on your face; it's an expression of not being worried or anxious. Moving through life with the greatest of ease is a reflection of the mental state of knowing it's done. Because we were not taught the correct use of our minds, we double-check God by re-praying for the same things over and over again. We act as if one time is not enough or God may not have heard us. As a matter of fact because I understand how to use my mind, I pray from my mind through my thoughts by focusing on the good that I want in my life and rejecting the bad. I work at not thinking about those things I don't want in my life because I don't want those things to manifest. To relax the mind in the present while waiting for the results to show up in our lives means we have to be in a "state of knowing" it is done. We are unable to rest our minds in the present moment if

145

we only believe because believing is hoping and hope is not strong enough. Hope may get us started but faith will sustain us all the way through. Just believing leaves the door cracked open for doubt to set in and take us off course mentally.

Faith knows. Believing hopes it works. Faith is mentally selling out to what we want, no matter the price we will have to pay emotionally. Faith doesn't get mad when no one helps; rather, it gets stronger because now we know how much we want what we want. Faith attracts everyone and everything we need to succeed.

Here is an example of how we use faith all the time without realizing it. When we drive our cars, we have faith that the brakes will work every time – we don't even think about it. Imagine how many people would drive if they had to think about whether or not the brakes would work. The roads would probably be empty because of fear and doubt. There would be no rush hour. This same concept should be used in the everyday occurrences of our lives. We must not worry about the results but know everything will work out. Why do we have so much faith in the "man-made" brakes, but so little faith in the use of our minds? The reason is that, we've driven our cars repeatedly and the brakes never failed us so we trust them every time. By the same token, we have made some mistakes in judgment over time so we believe our minds will let us down. There are brake failures but there are many more failures of the mind running rampant through our society. The brakes are mechanical devices that work most of the time; the mind is a spiritual entity that fails most of the time from ignorance. The mind must be trained and understood in order to use it as the positive force for which it was spiritually designed.

Many people pray for something in the morning and defeat it by lunch by the words that come out of their mouths. How do we learn how to operate in faith where we know before we see the results? Let's use the weightlifter analogy.

When the weightlifter begins lifting, he uses lightweights. The more he works out, the stronger he becomes. He is able to lift more weight with each trip to the gym. Faith is the muscle of the mind and it gets stronger the more we exercise it. As the weightlifter does with weights, we must begin with having faith in small things, let those small things become reality, and move to the larger areas of our lives. If the ideas or thoughts are too large and our faith is too small, we may give up at the first sign of struggle. Once faith grows and becomes unshakable, we can use it to produce the great things we are capable of producing in our lives because we have been ordained to do great things.

The next activity of the mind that chooses thoughts by faith is the Will.

The Will

The Will is the part of the mind that deals with thoughts about things. The Will never chooses the thing; rather, it chooses the thought about the thing. The only purpose of the Will is to accept or reject thoughts and, by doing so, directs mental and physical behavior. The goal is to learn how to accept the thoughts of what we want and reject the thoughts of what we don't want in our lives.

How does the Will know what thoughts to accept and which ones to reject? It knows by what we believe. The Will never randomly goes out and selects a thought without first looking at what we believe. If we believe in failure then it will choose all the thoughts that come into our minds that match with what we believe about failing and reject the winning ones. The same is true about winning. If you believe in winning then the Will chooses winning thoughts. Everything is connected to what we believe. Beliefs are the cornerstone of our lives. It is impossible to use the Will for good until we change our negative beliefs. Remember, the Will only chooses the thought about the thing; it does not chose the thing.

When we decide to eat, we don't choose the food but the thought about the food. If we had to physically see the food before we made a choice, we would have to visit every place we wanted to eat at before we chose. Because thoughts are alive, we can choose the thoughts about different kinds of foods and experience them in our minds before we buy them. The thought of fried chicken has a different sensation than the thought of roasted chicken; they're both chicken. Understanding this very fact was instrumental in my losing weight. When the thought of fried chicken came so did the sensation of how it tasted. That's where the struggle began. This is where changing what I believed about food helped me use my Will to win, instead of the roller coaster ride most folks take when losing weight. I ate for pleasure and ended up in physical pain because my Will chose what tasted good but wasn't good for my body. In my house, we had a candy bowl on the table – not a fruit bowl. When I changed the belief about food from pleasure to food for fuel, my body responded by dropping the weight. Notice I did not say I changed the food; rather, I changed the belief about the food and it resulted in a change of my eating habits. When I'm driving down the street, I don't smell vegetables, I smell KFC and that's when the mental battle ensues. If I'm mentally committed to changing how I look and feel then I will probably drive by. However, if my commitment is shaky, I will probably drive through to the pick-up window. It's so important to make this connection between the Will, Thoughts, and what we believe, if we expect to be successful at living. This process goes on all day, every day of our living existence on earth. Not understanding how to use the different parts of the mind makes it impossible to mind our own business, which is to run our lives.

The war for my life is fought on the battlefield of my mind. The only enemy is negative thoughts where winning or losing is determined by my Will. My life isn't mine but my choices are. My life is always changing as a direct result of new choices I make. Some of us are led to believe that we can give our Will to God and then take it back. The truth of the matter is that our Will is all ours and it cannot be given to God and then taken back. Because of erroneous teachings about the Will, many of us are stuck in this give-and-take scenario. What is meant by giving our Will to God is making our decisions by listening to our right mind or gut feelings which is God speaking to us. If we do good or bad, it is all our Will because it is our choice. When God created us with a Will, God put it totally under our control in order for us to be free. If God was supposed to make our choices, he would not have given us a Will. He could have made us like cats and dogs, driven by instincts with our nose to the ground.

If our lives are not going anywhere, it is not God's or the Devil's fault; the fault lies with the one who makes the choice. Without the Will, the process of evolution would cease to exist. Evolution cannot move forward without a new choice by a new creation. The creation is given something new through the use of spiritual insight, and it is the Will that makes it happen. There would be no need for faith, because we could not connect our thoughts. Without faith, it would not matter what we believed because we would have no way to control the process. Without the Will, the world would be more insane than it already is. No one would be able to reject negative thoughts or be able to acquire new information because the choice to read would not be available.

God gave us access to all of his power by the use of the Will; yet we suffer from disease, sickness, poverty, and despair. The reason is that we use our Will to choose thoughts of disease, sickness, poverty, and despair. We must begin to use our Will to choose thoughts of health, power, and prosperity, and this can only be done through new information to change what we believe.

Before I decided to write this book, I had to be thoroughly convinced of the power of the mind before I was willing to talk about it. I "caught"

Herpes as a result of buying sex. When I first found out, I would have outbreaks about every two months. My Will was selecting thoughts of disease. I started reading books on the power of the mind. I began selecting thoughts of health and rejecting thoughts of disease. At this time in my life, it has been over three years since I have had a Herpes outbreak. If you doubt me, try it for yourself. The only requirement for the power to work for you as it has for me is to have no doubt.

Now, we will move to the part of the mind that is used for recall of our past so that we might not keep repeating the same mistakes and that is the Ego.

The Ego

The Ego is simply memory of past physical experiences. It is our mental secretary. The Ego files every experience we've had under the headings, Pain or Pleasure. That which causes pain, it seeks a way to escape and that which causes pleasure, it runs to.

The Ego's purpose is to recall experiences from the past so that we do not repeat the things that keep us stuck. The Ego is a backward looking part of the mind. To move forward in life, we must understand the Ego so that we will begin to live.

The battle for our lives is between God and our Ego. God speaks with knowing and the Ego speaks with doubt. When we make decisions based on what happened in the past, we are operating from our Ego. The information the Ego sends out is old, it has already happened. The information God sends out is for right now because God works only in the present moment. There is no past or future in God, only eternally now. We ease God out by not listening to the spirit from within but following the pull of the Ego of the past. It tries to live from the past in the present moment by overriding the spiritual urgings that constantly stab at our awareness like a hot knife in butter. The Ego is our false sense of self that we have created from all of our past experiences. The problem is that we think it is the real us so we spend most of our lives acting like someone we're not. The Ego should be a part of our lives but it should not run our lives. Its role is strictly for recall.

How do we break the grip of the Ego? One way is to start listening to the unemotional voice of God from within. There is an acronym that I use to break the Ego. It is I.C.E. The "I" is for impress. Let us stop wasting valuable time trying to impress others – whether it is with looks, money, knowledge, or anything that we think impresses. The next is "C" which stands for compare. We are all born unique but too many of us will die copies because we compare ourselves to with one another. Of all the people in this world, there is no one just like you so nobody can be you but you. The "E" stands for effort. We don't have to be responsible for the results but we must be responsible for the effort.

Remember, the Ego is just for recall not to retard our growth.

Double Minded

Next, we will break down the mind into two parts: the conscious mind and the subconscious mind. The conscious mind operates in the physical world and is a part of our brain. The subconscious mind operates in the spiritual world and this is our connection to God.

The conscious mind has no memory; it just retrieves information from the physical world through our five senses and passes the information to the subconscious for action or storage. The subconscious mind has everything we need to know about our past, present, and future. Even if we can't readily remember it, everything is recorded in our subconscious mind. The conscious mind is the control center and the subconscious mind is the power source.

The conscious mind is the center that controls the power because it is where the Will, our Faith, and the Ego reside. Our beliefs, conscience, intuition, and imagination take up residency in our subconscious mind. The conscious mind controls the subconscious mind so, in order to change our lives, we must take control of our conscious mind. To do this, we must make conscious use of the Will to make the choices that will influence our conscious mind so that it sends different information to the subconscious mind so that new beliefs will be created. Once the new information becomes new beliefs, our conscious mind will instinctively choose the thoughts that are right for us.

When we begin the process of changing our belief system, we must consciously choose to read, write, or listen to new, positive information. We cannot put a book under our pillows and expect to be wise the next day. There also must be a change of people, places, and things because our environment shaped our belief system. This is why people who grew up on the West Coast act differently than people who grew up on the East Coast. The conscious environment is different. Be mindful that the conscious mind is a part of the brain and the brain is the physical part of the mind. Everything outside of us is filtered through our conscious mind and sent to our subconscious mind for storage as belief. We must use one of the attributes of the conscious mind – the Will – to choose different actions about the same thoughts that come to us so the subconscious mind can create a new reality. When we don't make a conscious choice to control our conscious mind through positive information, we lose control of the power of the subconscious mind. To lose control of the power of the subconscious mind is called insanity. Insanity is simply crazy thoughts and images that play on the screen of our minds without our permission that we act upon. The only difference between the person standing on the corner laughing and talking to himself and any one of us is that he lost control of his conscious mind. It's the conscious mind that accepts or rejects thoughts. We get crazy thoughts and images playing across the screen of our minds but because we still have control of our conscious mind, we push them out of our awareness by choice. When the conscious control of the mind is not working properly, the power of the subconscious mind becomes our source of reference from which to act. To act from that source is very unpredictable.

I would like to reiterate that the control is the conscious mind. The word conscious means an awakened state; not asleep. To be conscious is to be awake and aware. When we go to bed, the conscious part of the mind goes to bed too; it is turned off. We cannot use our Will to choose what dreams to dream once we're asleep. That is done by the subconscious mind that sends out whatever it sends. Sometimes it's a dream of fame and fortune; other times, a nightmare. The subconscious mind is P.O.M. – Play Only Memory. It plays whatever it wants and whenever it wants to. When was the last time your subconscious mind sent a thought of something crazy that made you say, "Where did that come from?" Nobody can control the subconscious mind but we can all control our conscious mind. It is through the correct use of the conscious mind that we use the subconscious mind for good and not evil.

As stated earlier, the parts associated with the conscious mind are the Will, our Ego, and our Faith. The parts associated with the subconscious mind are the Conscience, Imagination, Intuition, Beliefs, and the Spirit of God. Thoughts are not in either category because they are associated with both because thoughts are the connection between the two. It is through thought that everything becomes real, from the unseen to the seen.

Goal-Mind

The reason goals are in this chapter on the mind is that it is how we focus our conscious mind to achieve great things. Achieving goals is not what goal setting is about; rather, it is the person we become on our way to the goal that is the lesson. People who have set goals and attained them know that, once it is done there are no rockets blaring in the air or any parties being thrown. They know it is time to set another goal so the process of achievement continues.

Our conscious mind needs something on which to focus the power of the subconscious mind. If it has nothing to go after, it will turn inward and begin to destroy the person. The saying, "An idle mind is the devil's workshop" is true to some extent. More aptly put, it's not a devil's workshop but the workshop of inactivity that creates evil. The mind is such a powerful force that, if it is not directed toward something positive, it will follow the path of least resistance. That path is negativity.

Not to set goals is like taking a trip without travel plans. How can we know where we're going or how long it will take to get there? Goals are dreams with a deadline. To dream and not put a time of achievement on it is just wishful thinking.

My very first goal was to read 20 minutes a day for 30 days just to create the habit of reading and it worked. Now, I love to read. I think everybody who doesn't like to read should set this as a goal because, without new information, there can't be a new choice. Goals help us stay focused and create good habits like consistency, commitment, and stick-ability. If something is not a habit, we won't do it. Setting goals doesn't have to be a physical achievement; it can be a mental achievement like creating the habit of reading on a regular basis. When I put a deadline on the dream of writing a book, it made me focus my energy to obtain the objective. Now that I understand the power of my mind and how focusing is just faith in action, I have written down my goals, laminated them, and taped them to my dashboard. When anyone gets in my vehicle, it looks like a billboard. I get some good feedback and some bad feedback, but my goals are for my mind – not theirs.

Mindset is important because whatever we set our minds on will grow. Whatever we ignore will die. Goals help us to set our minds on what we want. Let's stop traveling through life without travel plans. Set goals.

161

Let's Put It All Together

It's time to merge together all the parts of the mind to work as a whole.

When we are born, the first part of the mind that is activated is the conscious mind or soul. We don't have any beliefs or an Ego because those parts are developed as a result of accumulated physical information. The conscious mind or soul is an analyzing, categorizing, and distinguishing part of the mind. Its main purpose is to view information received from the outside world and associate an action with a reaction, or associate things with sensation. A baby cries when it's hungry. Mother feeds the baby and the conscious mind associates crying with being fed. When the baby is wet, it cries. Mother changes the diaper. Before you know it, baby cries for everything because it has associated crying with getting what it wants. (How many grown-up babies do we know who are still whining today?) This association is stored in the subconscious mind as beliefs. This is the beginning of the creation of the Ego, which is the memory of past physical experience.

Now faith, which is focusing on a thought with our beliefs until it manifests in our lives, is used but with unawareness of its power. As a child, we focus on the thoughts of the things we want regardless of how inconvenient it is to others. And faith makes it so. It's what we call "baby needs" – we want what we want when we want it. The Will is always used because it's our ability to choose. Without a Will, we would not be mentally free. As we grow, so do our belief system and Ego. The belief system is always a reflection of the environment in which the conscious mind or soul lives. That's why a person born in the South will act differently than a person born in the North. Until we understand the environment in which we were raised in we will never understand ourselves. We leave home with our beliefs in tow and our Ego activated. We find that the world is nothing like the environment we grew up in so the Ego tries to compensate for it by creating another person we call ourselves. It is our public self and the private self lives just below the surface of our conscious mind. We begin to live as our public self so much that it causes internal pain from the private self that wants to get out.

163

This is the beginning of addiction – two heads trying to live as one.

These two selves are the result of the internal battle for control of the mind fought by the Ego and the spirit. The Ego wins most of the time because it has experience on its side and spirit doesn't. Things that are experienced leave a deeper impression than things that have not been experienced. When God alerts us to what's happening at this moment, we don't listen because the Ego is also calling and it has a knowing from past experiences. This is how we ease God out of our minds. We turn to the past for the answers to right now. The Ego gets its information from our belief system which is a result of our environment that was created through the conscious mind.

Last but not least are thoughts. Which are self-contained because no one can stop or start the stream of thoughts from coming into their heads. Thoughts are the interface between what we believe and what God creates in our physical life.

Now that I've put it all together, the common denominator in the working of all the parts is the understanding of how they work together as a whole.

Exercise

We must work out to help work it out.

Exercise is one of the only things that makes me feel good and is good for me. I don't exercise just to lose physical weight but to relieve mental weight that accumulates from stress. Exercise should be a part of the healing process as a mental and emotional outlet. Instead of renting X-rated movies to relieve stress, I go to the gym. Now exercise should not be a fix-all; rather, it should be part of the process of changing your life. Exercise takes time and taking too much time in any one area may cause you to neglect other areas. Exercise can become an addiction just like anything and create problems in other areas of your life. The best thing about exercise is that it relieves stress by moving oxygen through the body, which has a cleansing affect. There's something about oxygen that allows us to release through it the things we could not say. (That's the whole concept behind counting to ten while breathing deeply before we act – it is the oxygen.)

Through exercise, confession, confronting, and feeding my mind, I was able to get off of Prozac. If we let our physical house crumble, our spirit is not able to accomplish anything. Once the body breaks down we go broke trying to fix it. A broken body is a burden to the world and to God because without the use of a strong vessel we cannot manifest our purpose.

Please start an exercise program, along with nutritional understanding of food. Taking care of you means total responsibility for the physical as well as the mental.

13

GOD MISUNDERSTOOD

IT IS VERY IMPORTANT that we have a better understanding of God. There can never be freedom without understanding preceding it.

God is the changeless in the changeable, the invisible in the visible. The foundation of our life must be built on the truth of *God in mankind* not God and mankind. As long as we perceive God as being everywhere but inside of us, we will continue to be prisoners of ignorance.

All my life, I was taught about "the man upstairs." There isn't any man or upstairs. *God is!* God is spirit, truth, and is everywhere at the same time. God is in every one of us. God is the intelligence behind everything. He keeps the sun shining and the grass growing without any help from us. The same intelligence that holds the world together is the same intelligence that's inside of all humankind. The next time you go outside, look up and notice that the world is inside of nothing. God – the intelligence behind everything – keeps everything in order.

My whole perception of God was built from misunderstandings. The people who taught me what they believed to be the truth merely passed along information somebody told them. They never verified it through reading or research. The word research means "to search again; to go back and look at the facts." Once this is done, we can make a decision based on what we've found. Research is important because each of us can read the same books and perceive the information differently. In order to take ownership – to be responsible – we must stop putting our lives on the line based on someone else's perception.

For me, it took losing everything before I became willing to do some research. Through research of other religions, *I found new information* – which made me dismiss some of the things I'd been taught. What I was taught about God wasn't working in my life. It's still not working for those who initially taught me. Throughout my life, I was scared to form my own belief about God so it was easier to fit in and go with the flow.

The Church I went to became a place for emo-
tionalism, not spiritual understanding. I was
caught up in the shouting and singing but my life
was still full of fear and pain. It became a place
where no one had an understanding of how to live
so we kept doing the same things looking for different results and on Sunday we cried about it.
Worshiping God should be a way of life, *not* a
one-day-a-week experience. Through my
research, I learned that worshiping God was to do
something good with my life and know that God
did it all through me. I know a lot of people who
believe in God but don't believe in themselves.
So we have a whole lot of poor people who know
how to pray and not prosper. I began to go to God
on the inside of myself because that's where the
Kingdom of Heaven is. If we want to know God,
we must start by getting to know ourselves and
God will be revealed through us. God is you spiritually, meaning *the spirit that is in you is God.*
The part that is you is your soul.

Think about it. When God created mankind, he
did not create a new spirit for each and every one
of us but he *put all of his spirit* into each and every
one of us. We are divinely made but few of us will

ever understand the power that lives within so we go through life feeling and living powerless.

Humankind is God's connection to the earth through the mind. When I realized that everything I needed to be successful in this life I already had within me, and that I only needed to develop it to be great, my life took off in a new direction. It's not that I am great; rather, the *God in me* is great and I am merely the beneficiary of this greatness.

We are here to serve God but we must come to a knowing that God serves us too. If the world doesn't change through us who else will God use? All things put on this earth are for humankind to use, so who's serving whom? The sun shines, the fruit grows, the fish are in the sea, and the moon glows at night. This is for *our* benefit. Physically we are different but spiritually we are all the same. There isn't anyone greater or lesser than each of us, spiritually. Until we bring our understanding up to the level of Jesus the Christ, we will never be able to manifest the things Christ did.

I believe the things I say may be going against the grain of the masses but, if you look at the world around us, there's too much suffering. The guys who flew the planes into the World Trade Center and the Pentagon on *9/11* prayed 5 times a day but they *still* killed a lot of people just to make a statement. I believe it is important to understand that Islam, Christianity, Hinduism, and Buddhism are philosophies chosen to live by; *it is not* the individual. We are spiritual beings with human conditions and our responsibility is to bring Heaven on earth through finding and living our purpose. When we label ourselves with these philosophies, this tends to make us take sides and that causes separation. Everybody needs a philosophy to live by but we must learn to be tolerant of each other's philosophy. God did not create mankind to be the same. Look at the number of languages we have in the world. If we were supposed to be the same, why not speak one tongue?

Intolerance is the root to all evil in this world. When we only learn one spiritual philosophy, we become narrow minded. We can only filter our experiences through what we know. If we know only one way to live, we tend to reject other people as being wrong or lost. I'm not a member of any organized group but I am a member of life so that allows me to think for myself. That is why God gave us a mind.

I decided to tap into some of the other religious philosophies and this helped me create a greater cosmic view. I read books on Hinduism, Buddhism, and Islam. I really enjoy eastern philosophy because it talks about the power within and how the mind is the place where this power is accessible. Also that God lives in us and through our minds, he creates with our bodies. When I look at the order that God created things, I noticed that *he created man last*. If that's true how can man know what God did in the beginning? There are two ways to answer this question. One, man is making one awesome guess, or two, God is in us so we were there too.

Through research, one of the things that came to my awareness was that, when God created mankind, he was re-creating himself on earth. This is why the Bible says we were created in the spiritual image of God with the rights to use the power of God through our minds. Genesis 1:26–28 is where God talks about the power given to mankind to use in order to create. Genesis 1:26, says:

"And God said; Let us make man in our
image, after our likeness: and let them
have dominion over the fish of the sea,
and over the fowl of the air, and over the
cattle, and over all the earth, and over
every creeping thing that creepeth upon
the earth."

What we need to understand in this verse is
that God gave mankind power over the physical
world and everything in it, on it, and under it. It
means that we are responsible for the physical
world including our own physical life. So, if anything is going to change in our lives or in the
world, we will have to change it.

I went to Church most of my life but I was
never taught where I fit into *God's plan*. Too
many of us are waiting for God to change our
lives because we were never taught that it is *our*
job, not God's. The result is wasting our lives,
wishing and hoping things will change. God gave
us the power to change our own lives. If this were
not true, why did he give us *free will*? When I
decided to lose weight, I did not send God to the
gym while I stayed home and watched TV. I had
to consistently get up and go to the gym. When I

went back to school at the age of 31, I did not send God to class, I had to show up.

In Genesis 1:26, the word *dominion* is used. Dominion means "to have supreme authority or control." The word *supreme* means "highest in power, authority, or rank." We are the highest authority of anything on the earth but we continue to live below our potential because of bad information and misinformation – which is information someone else passed on without research and investigation.

This chapter is to help us understand our place in the world so that we might stop being out of place. As long as the head is out of place, everything else will be displaced or misplaced. This is where religion is failing the world. Religion puts too much emphasis on *having service* instead of *being of service*. We cannot be of service if we don't know our place in the scheme of things.

Now, let's take a look at Genesis 1:27. This passage says:

> "So God created man in his own image,
>   in the image of God created he him;
>   male and female created he them."

The thing we must focus on is the part where it says, "Created he him." We need to say this out loud a few times until the understanding comes. What this means is that God created himself on the earth, and male and female is how he created himself. Simply put, *we are God in quality* but *not* *in magnitude*. The word *quality* means "an essential character or nature." *Essential* means "constituting or part of the nature of something." So, the quality of God means we have the nature of God and the power of God within. The word *magnitude* means "great in extent or size." Since we are not God in magnitude, we cannot control the whole world; however, we can control *our* world.

Bad information from our childhood makes us live disconnected from our true nature, which is divine. Because God is spirit, he uses us as his vessels. This is the reason mankind was created. *We are his interface* on the earth; *we are his way* from the spiritual to the physical. God put all of his spirit in us and gave us a mind and brain so that we might evolve toward an oneness with him on earth. Because we are more physically inclined, we tend to think that the physical world

175

is the only reality. The physical world *is not* the real reality at all because it changes with the times. The real reality is that of spirit – of God – that manifests physical things out of itself. Every person on earth is a center of creation and we create by our beliefs through the thoughts we choose and the faith we connect to those thoughts. It doesn't matter if it's good or bad, right or wrong; the spirit just creates what we send out through our thoughts.

Now, let's move to Genesis 1:28. This passage says:

> "And God blessed them, and God said
> unto them, Be fruitful, and multiply,
> and replenish the earth, and subdue it:
> and have dominion over the fish of the
> sea, and over the fowl of the air, and
> over every living thing that moveth on
> the earth."

Because we never understood our true nature which is to create, replenish, have dominion, and subdue the earth, we are destroying both the earth and ourselves. Let's break down this verse so that we might get a clearer understanding of what it is saying. Look first at the word *blessed* as it pertains to this verse. *Blessed* means that God empowered us to rule over the earth – he did *not empower us* to rule over each other. We fail to realize that the same seed of power that is planted in me is also planted in you. This is why we have so many uprisings and rebellions. *Mankind is trying to rule over the wrong things* while destroying the things he should rule over on earth.

I hear folks say, "I'm blessed" all of the time but they don't really understand the power connected to that word. If they did, their lives would be better. That phrase has become a cliché. The power of it is lost because everybody is saying it simply because everybody else is saying it. I go and get my morning coffee and cordially speak to someone. One person responds, "I'm blessed," I want to say "shut-up" because I see that their life is in shambles. Being blessed is not just about waking up; rather, it is more about making a difference in the world. If your life is *out of control, then* you don't understand what it means to be blessed. One of the biggest SINS in the world is for a person to choose to sit by idly and do nothing with all of the power of God inside of them.

They choose to waste away in shame and self-pity. To be *blessed* is about what I do, *not* what I say.

I met a homeless guy one wintry day. He was begging for change so I decided to stop and talk with him. When I asked, "How are you doing," he responded, "I'm blessed." He then went on to say that people had been trying to steal his joy all day. I said to myself, who wants to take something from a guy with nothing, begging for change in the winter? This goes to show how clichés can keep you in denial. We must understand where we are in life and not cover it up with words that have become a fad.

Now, let's deal with "to be fruitful and multiply." This is a highly misunderstood statement. Being fruitful means to make something grow out of your life; that's it…that's all. Many of us were led to believe that it meant to have a lot of children. We took it literally and used no common sense, so we have so many children until we find ourselves in poverty. When it says to multiply, it can mean to multiply your business or your spiritual life. It's just plain common sense to me that, if I have two children and I'm struggling to provide for them, why would I bring a third child into the world to make the struggle more difficult? There are so many of us whose parents did not use common sense, had a lot of children, and caused the entire family to grow up poor. Remember, poverty breeds insanity.

The last part of verse 1:28 that I will address is the replenishing of the earth – something we are not doing. As a matter of fact, we are *de*-plenishing the earth. We over build, over hunt, over fish, and over eat. These cause a lot of human waste that we bury in the earth. So, our dominion over the earth is true to form *except* we're going the wrong way. How can we start a turn around? Well, one of the ways is to start teaching spirituality in school. Churches need to stop teaching praise and worship and begin to teach how to live. Things like managing a checkbook, eating right, sharing of pain to heal the mind, just to name a few life skills, should be taught *both* in churches and schools.

Our children need some honesty from us so-called grown ups about how it was when we were their age. Mankind is the steward of the earth and because the steward is mentally and emotionally ill, everything under the steward will suffer. Life is a gift from God and what we do with it is our gift to him. The only way God can bring his blessings to the world is through us because we are his point of contact on the earth.

If you want to give God thanks, *do something with your life*. God doesn't need lip service; the world needs doers. Remember…what *you do* speaks so loudly, folks can't hear what you say! *I can't hear what you're saying because your life is so LOUD*.

We need to understand that *the He that is in me is greater than the he that is in the world*. For a long time I was led to believe that *the he* that was *in me was God* and "the he" that was in the world was the devil. There's only one power and, when we learn to use it to its full potential, it will reward us. Conversely, if we misuse that power, it will punish us. There's only one power that makes everything out of itself. When we misunderstand statements like the ones noted, we will be stuck in the middle of a holy war between God and the world.

Let me break it down so that you might be able to use it properly and get rewarded. *The he that is in me is the spirit of God* and "the he" that is in the world is my physical body. Our struggles come when we are taught that we must fit into the physical world but are not taught about our place in the spiritual world. We have all heard sayings like "the mind is willing but the flesh is weak." This kind of teaching will have us in constant conflict with ourselves. There is nothing wrong with our bodies; our bodies were not made to guide our lives. The purpose of the body is to express a spiritual idea and, once the idea is fully expressed, there is no need for the body anymore. We are all spiritual ideas trying to be expressed through physical bodies. Far too many of us will die with our ideas never expressed because we choose to stick with the old information, that which has been taught to us, and not work to discover our purpose. Neither Fort Knox nor The Federal Reserve is the richest place in the country; rather, it is the graveyard. The graveyard is full of unexpressed spiritual ideas that could have possibly changed the world or, at least, changed a family's legacy. We are the greatest thieves in our lives. We continue to steal from ourselves and don't realize that anything is missing. We steal from ourselves when we refuse to find our purpose and live up to that potential. All of us have been given a piece of the same puzzle; however, the puzzle cannot be finished until everyone brings their piece to the table of life. Because of bad information and misinformation, both of which cause fear and doubt, many of us have thrown our pieces to the side because we have given up on ourselves. *Potential is untapped power* that lies dormant inside of us until we choose to activate it. Our greatness is calling. But few will answer that call. The majority of us will settle for less and whine about *more*. So, "the he" that is in the world is the physical body and we cannot continually condemn a part of us and expect to be whole. The key is to learn to bring the spirit and body into harmony through the mind so that we can live to our full potential and express our purpose. A life guided by the body will self-destruct in a matter of time but a life guided by the spirit becomes a powerful existence.

One of our problems is that we are socialized, *not spiritualized,* so we live from the outside, in. To be socialized means that we are taught how to fit into the physical world and that's the reason we live from the outside in. English, math, and history will do me no good at 3 AM when I'm looking to do "the wrong thing." It's only through knowledge of both worlds, along with knowledge of self, that I will have a chance to overcome any struggle. To be spiritualized means that we are aware of our connection to the Spirit of God that lives within our minds. Just like the world socialized us through the use of physical information, we must spiritualize ourselves through the use of spiritual information. The world socialized us but it will not spiritualize us. Since we live in two worlds at the exact same time (the spiritual and the physical), the mind is the place where we choose which one will guide us. It is our responsibility and, if we fail to do it, suffering will continue to be the outcome of that ignorance.

When I talk about spiritual information, I'm not just talking about the Bible. Spiritual information is any information that teaches life principles. I believe that the Bible may be too painful a book to begin with because, given what we've been taught up to this point, it may make us dislike ourselves or become self-righteous.

God created the purpose for my life and then physically created me to fulfill it. This is why *I* *had to go through what I had to <u>grow</u> through* in order to be the person I am today. What you go through is for you and no one else. Don't get stuck in the past but realize there is a purpose for everything – nothing happens in God's world by mistake. Everything in life is useable; it either pushes you forward or holds you back; it's all in how you look at it.

To live our lives not trying to find our purpose means our existence will be full of strife and pain. Many people are dying because they have nothing to live for. We watch what we eat but never find out what's eating us. We keep trying to answer spiritual questions from a material perspective. If we don't know our purpose, we must work to create one by trying different things until we find our fit. If we only do what we know, we will never know what we can do. It is through living our purpose that we truly express the power of God. Not knowing ourselves will make us believe that God gave out gifts and missed us. Everybody has at least one thing that they're good at and that's the purpose of your life – to do that one thing you're good at.

There are things in my life that I will be struggling with for the rest of my life; however, I will not let those things dominate all of my life. Let us not get overwhelmed with overcoming every bad habit; rather, let us be sure to continue moving forward. There isn't a person, rich or poor, who is not struggling with something. The key is not to let the struggle be our only mission in life. Don't get caught up with thinking that we separate ourselves from God through sin. Sin is the *only* road to truth. Had I not done some sinful things in my life, I would still be lost. Think about it: *how can we separate ourselves from something that's everywhere at the same time and all of it is in all places?* When we sin, we mentally stop listening to that still, constant voice of conscience, which is God. As a result, we destroy ourselves.

Traditional religion kept me stuck for a long time so I decided to ask, "Why?" I asked *why* because everything I believed came from someone else – someone I observed who did not practice what was preached – and, to my knowledge, those individuals never studied or did research. Just asking the question will begin to open the doors of our minds for new answers to old problems.

Remember that the person who never asks a new question can never get a new answer.

Stop Blaming The Devil

As emotional prisoners, it is important to stop blaming the devil for the condition of our lives. As long as we have something to blame for not changing our lives, we cannot grow. Our problem is with *the evil in our hearts* caused by errors in judgment due to bad information or mis-information picked up from our childhood.

Blaming the devil is our excuse for not under- standing the evil that lies within each of us. The devil can't make us do anything because our Will is free. We must be conscious and responsible for our choices.

The devil did not sell me crack cocaine, make me buy sex, or max out my credit cards. I did it to myself trying to feel good for the moment –and because I had no knowledge of self and ignored my first mind, *I made those bad choices.*

One Sunday, I remember listening to a pastor say that the devil tried to get him by putting him in the hospital with high blood pressure and problems with his blood sugar. This guy looked to be at least 100 pounds overweight and, if he moved too quickly, all of the buttons on his suit would become unidentified flying objects. I was shocked to see how many people agreed with him. It did not appear that anybody in the congregation that day considered that it was all the fried chicken, biscuits, Chinese food, and no exercise that was pastor's problem. I hear people blame the devil for their car breaking down. It could be that we drive the car all the time and breaking down is a part of usage. If we really stopped to consider it, we could not fathom the amount of time wasted fighting and blaming the devil for our problems. If our lives are in shambles, we must accept that responsibility. If our lives do not go anywhere, the fault lies with the person who makes the choices.

The devil made me do it is no defense if you do a crime, go to court, and tell that to the Judge. I promise you that the Judge will not let you off. He would probably say, "Both of you can serve this time together."

Our struggle is not with the devil but with good and evil on the inside of ourselves. If two dogs were fighting, one was good and the other evil, which one would win? The one you feed the most. If we feed the good part of ourselves, we do Godly things. If we feed the evil part of ourselves, we do devilish things. We can be Godly one moment and devilish the next. It depends on what information we're operating on at that moment. In the "Our Father prayer," it says *deliver us from evil*. Evil is bad information that causes errors in judgment. Because we internalize the information as truth, we do evil things because of evil beliefs. Let me show you how evil is the problem based on personal experience.

As a child, I watched how the women in my life treated men. As a result, I picked up bad information about women and internalized it as truth. *My truth* was that women were no good; they were only after a man's money. As a teenager, I began to have relationships with girls with the belief that they were no good. I entered these relationships with evil in my heart and my mind. Did I treat those girls with respect, or with abuse and humiliation? It was the latter. I believed that women were just sex objects for me to use for my own gratification. *Here's the setup:* I got into a relationship with a female. In the beginning, I treated her like a queen. Once I got the sex, the real me came out and I began to treat her badly. I did not answer her calls; I did not want to be bothered unless I wanted more sex. Now, since I am the first guy with whom she's had a relationship, she internalizes the way I treated her as men are no good then judges other men by what I did to her.

Hurt causes pain and pain leaves scars. The scars are so deep that we need protection so we put up a wall and isolate ourselves from the world while at the same time trying to live from behind the wall. Evil is the outcome of putting up the wall and never letting anyone in or letting ourselves out. The girls I hurt leave the relationship with mental and emotional scars and put up a wall. They begin to abuse men, themselves, or both. The new guy she abuses leaves their relationship hurt and his wall goes up. He, in turn, abuses women, himself, or both. This cycle repeats over and over again until we end up where we are right now – a world full of hurt people hurting each other, trying to live from behind the wall.

This is just one of many beliefs I had to change in order to stop sending out evil through my actions because of bad information turned into negative beliefs. If each of us would assume the responsibility to investigate our belief systems and make the necessary changes, evil would begin to vanish and love will flourish. The world became evil one person at a time. Change for the good is made one person at a time as well.

Another reason evil is so wide spread is the irresponsibility of the mass media. We are constantly bombarded with the evil deeds of evildoers. The good news is always last. There is "bad" in the best of us; there is "good" in the worst of us. I got a call from the local newspaper asking me to buy a subscription. My response was that good news doesn't sell so why buy bad news. The salesperson on the other end of the phone broke out into an agreeing laugh. We buy the bad-news newspaper and watch the negatively focused news on television. This stuff feeds our subconscious to the point that we begin to be so afraid of dying that we forget to live. We begin to believe that the world is messed-up and resign ourselves to "there's nothing I can do about it".

The world is fine; it's the people who are messed-up. Evil would not exist if mankind did not exist. Mankind is God's only creation that lives in the constant battle between good and evil. Human beings are the only ones who can perceive or comprehend whether or not there is a God. Let's choose to get off of the battlefield in our souls, believe in God, and let life take its course.

Where Is Heaven and Hell?

I've spent a great deal of my life trying to live right so I might go to "Heaven" and avoid "Hell." Through reading and research, I have come to realize it's not just a place; rather, it's states of mind. Both are internal states of being; a way of thinking. I can make a Heaven out of Hell or a Hell out of Heaven by what I believe and the thoughts I choose to act on.

Part of the "Our Father" says, "...Thy kingdom come, thy will be done on earth as it is in Heaven." Where are we trying to go when Heaven is coming here? Many gospel songs relate to "the sweet by and by." Because we do not understand ourselves or why we are here, we choose to suffer now with the hope of paradise later. How do we "walk around heaven all day" without a phys-

191

ical body? We need to stop waiting to die to go to Heaven while missing life on earth. All there is, at this moment, is *now*. Of all the people who died, none came back to tell us what it's like on the other side. Too many of us are so heavenly bound, we are no earthly good. We have bought into the belief that suffering is *the ticket* to get to Heaven. All through my life, people tried to scare me with going to Hell if I didn't straighten up. My response was that I might as well have all the fun I can before I go. Because of that belief, I smoked all the drugs that I could get my hands on, had sex with all the girls who would let me; I cheated, stole, and manipulated my way through life. My behavior came to a crashing halt when I realized that Heaven and Hell were not just places; rather, states of mind where the only thing that mattered was what I believed.

Hell feels like being unloved, having no self-respect, and living in fear, worry, and doubt – it is being afraid of everything. Heaven feels like love of self and love for others with the understanding that there is only one spirit that invades the being of everything so we are all connected.

Not only are we connected to everything that's alive and breathing, we are also connected to our environment including the air, water, trees, and animals. *The Father's Will* is done on earth as it is in Heaven through believing in ourselves, having the courage to be different, and taking risks to make things happen. There's nothing that will be done on earth without coming through humankind. To live our purpose is to bring Heaven to earth. To live outside of our nature turns earth into Hell.

It makes no sense for any of us to spend our entire lives working to overcome all of the stuff other people forced upon us in our childhoods, only to physically die and burn for rest of eternity because we could not get it right.

Remember, Heaven and Hell are not just a *physical* place; rather, states of mind where the only determinant of the one we live in is our beliefs.

14

FINANCIAL I.Q.

FINANCIAL I.Q. MEANS JUST WHAT IT SAYS, getting knowledge of how money works. We are taught how to get a job and earn money but few of us are taught how to make money work for us. If you don't think money has anything to do with being an emotional prisoner, take note of how you feel when you're broke versus when you just got paid. I would venture to say that most of us don't do well when we're broke. It is stressful and depressing. Money is a *mood changer* and don't let anyone tell you different. We live in a country where money rules. Through learning to understanding money, and how to manage my money, it keeps me mentally stable in that area.

We don't walk past the guy who is begging for change because he's not human – he bleeds like us and will die like us. We walk by him because he's broke and when you're broke you have nothing coming. We don't even make eye contact, hoping the beggar won't ask for our money because it is a painful reminder of what could happen to us if we don't get our financial houses in order. In this country, we can have the ability to heal the sick or walk on water but, if our bank account says *zero,* we will suffer.

In the Bible it talks about the love of money is the root to all evil. The lack of money plants evil roots, too. The overwhelming majority of the people who break into cars, rob banks or other people at gunpoint, and commit crimes, are not millionaires. Understand that we are *threefold beings:* mental, physical, and spiritual. Money is a vital part of our physical existence, so we must understand how it works in order to develop fully as a physical being.

Many of us spend our lives trying to know God; yet, we neglect the physical knowledge about finances that we need know to be whole. To seek only information about God has left a lot of us so physically poor that we become burdens to our children. Without financial freedom there cannot be physical freedom. We spend too many of our quality years working on someone else's dream. When we work for someone else, it keeps *the other person's* dream alive. If a job were the answer, the paycheck would take care of our bills, right? We work all of our lives, only to retire into poverty. We are taught to be consumers, not owners; investors, not traders; and homeowners, not real estate investors. School systems nationwide should have classes dealing with entrepreneurship, money, investments, and financial planning. Since these kinds of classes *are not* being taught, too many of us leave school, go to college, get into debt, and end up sacrificing our entire lives on "the installment plan."

Ignorance about money will not lessen the pain that comes with emotional spending. I'm constantly talking to people about going to the library and picking up books on investing, real estate, and tax shelters. No one has called me in reference to any of the books I recommended but they continue to call to complain about their lives. I grew up poor and was taught poor habits. Through educating myself, I made the decision that I will not die poor. When I decided to write this book, I bought a book on *how to* write a book. I self-published and I promote my own book. I understood the financial benefit of doing it myself. I get all the money not a small percentage.

I dropped out of school in the 8th grade. As I look back at my life, I can see a reward for doing that. The reward is that I have not been programmed to get a job, start a family, buy a house, and die broke. I'm not saying education is bad but it is *sorely lacking* when it comes to the subjects of finance and spirituality. If money is not important enough to be taught in school, stop and think about the suffering we go through because of the lack of it. Having money allows us to see better doctors, drive better cars, live in better houses, and be of help to others. Knowledge of money is crucial because money ranks up there with oxygen. We have to have it to live.

When was the last time you went to church and no one asked for tithes and offerings? We pay taxes to earn money, and then we pay taxes to spend the money we earn. We pay to be born and we pay when we die. Learning about money has allowed me to break the payday-to-payday cycle many of us live in today. Folks say God changes everything. Stay broke and watch how much you suffer. God gave us the ability to change things through choice.

Nobody ever taught me about money. On one of my many trips to the library to get some spiritual books, a book on investing grabbed my attention like a magnet. At that moment, I decided to put down my spiritual books and check out books about money. Having a spiritual understanding, along with a physical mastering of life, has made me a powerful person.

Understanding the spiritual world keeps me humble. Because the only thing I do is choose; then God creates my choices. Understanding the physical world, which includes finances, helps me do the Will of God on earth. I have big dreams of opening up a treatment center, not just for drugs but for all addictions; other goals include opening a childcare facility and a computer learning academy. These things require money. There are people who have made lots of money in their lives – doctors, lawyers, movie stars, and sports heroes – but they didn't know what to do with it. They spent it on things and today are broke.

We go to college to learn how to work for money. It's time to learn how to make money work for us. Take time out of your busy lives and do yourself a favor. Learn how money works. Money is an idea. When we find our ideas – *our purpose* – and pursue them, money will come our way. Let us stop trying to make a living and *live our making, which will make our living.*

Folks always ask me where to start and I say go to the Library. Few ever get started and fewer will finish. They get excited with my talk but once the emotional aspect leaves, they revert back to ignorance. Decide to be a *doer*; not a talker. The world is full of noisemakers. The only thing that separates the winners from the losers is the choice to take action.

15

LAWS OF THE UNIVERSE

THERE ARE SPIRITUAL LAWS that govern the universe and apply to our everyday lives. The laws are set by God and upheld by mankind. We have two sets of laws under which we live. There are physical laws made by man that can be changed by veto or vote, and there are spiritual laws set by God that cannot be changed.

I'm writing about the laws of the universe because we suffer when we break the laws. A lack of understanding of how the laws work makes them work against us. I stumbled across these laws as a direct result of my search for the truth about life. The spiritual laws are how God works in and through us. Spiritual laws don't create anything; they tell how the spirit creates. When we break this law we pay with our lives. There is only one power and one set of spiritual laws. When we understand these laws, we produce great lives. When we don't, it leads to pain and suffering. The only thing the spirit does is create our beliefs through our thoughts; it's a law. You become what you think about.

Everything must first be sent out into the universe as a thought before it can become a thing. Thoughts attached with faith moves God to create. The Bible says "so as a man thinketh and believeth in his heart so shall it be unto him." The heart that's referenced here is not the one beating in your chest. It is the heart of our minds – our beliefs. The reason Jesus lived such a power-filled life was because of his understanding of the laws that govern the universe. He tried to teach others but their mental eyes were blind and their spiritual ears were deaf. They looked but could not see; they listened but could not hear the truth. Not understanding the spiritual laws that govern the physical world means that we will never be able to live in our divinity nor have a fruitful life. What are some of the laws that govern life?

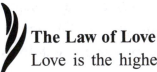

The Law of Love
Love is the highest and most supreme law there is. It is also the least understood.

Without love, life is difficult and confusing. Love is to life like blood is to the heart. We cannot live without it. We are born with the need for love but not with the knowledge of *how to* love. We must be taught how to give and receive it or else we enter life with a void in our souls. Note that I said we are born with *the need* for love because there is a difference between *a need* and a want. If we don't get what we *want*, we can live without it. If we don't get what we *need*, we cannot survive. *Love is a need* not a want. Giving love is important but receiving it is more important because we cannot give away something that we don't have.

When we are born, we cannot give love but we need to receive it in order to grow mentally and emotionally. This is where many of us become mentally and emotionally under fed. *I overeat because I was under fed* may sound like a paradox but it is not. I overate food to try to fill the void of being under fed love. Most mental and emotional problems can be traced back to the frustration of not getting enough love. If you want to make someone dysfunctional, you don't have to beat or holler at them; just don't love them.

Love is such a powerful thing that most of us leave home in need of it. So we go on a search looking for something that feels like love. When love is absent, it leaves a void and all voids must be filled. The crazy thing about love is that we don't know that its love we are looking for. This is like looking for a pair of new shoes at a computer store – they cannot be found. We've heard the saying "Looking for love in all the wrong places." For me, some of those places were the crack house, the prostitute's house, and sometimes the jailhouse. It doesn't matter how rich or poor we are, the void feels the same. There cannot be *true* freedom without love.

In the Bible, it talks about loving our neighbors as we love ourselves. I usually stopped at the "neighbor" part because I did not know how to love myself. For me, loving my neighbor was really people-pleasing because I had no knowledge of love. Love is not automatically fed into our minds as we grow through life. If we did not receive it as a child, we're probably not getting it now. The only way to get love is for us to give it to ourselves through feeding our minds good things about us. Along with this, we must physical start to take care of ourselves. We cannot truly love anyone without first loving ourselves.

Why is learning to love ourselves so hard? When we don't love ourselves, we create all kinds of bad habits in an attempt to fill the void where love should have been. Those bad habits will make us hate ourselves and we end up in a vicious cycle of loving and hating ourselves. It's important for us to stop beating up on ourselves. We must work to have some compassion and understanding about why we do what we do. Hate can never heal; it is a prison. Love will always wipe the slate clean.

When we begin this process of learning to love ourselves, we must set limits in our lives as to how far we will go and how far we will let others take us. We must stop saying "yes" when we really want to say "no." We must stop taking care of everyone else's needs while leaving our needs unmet. Learning to love ourselves means we take full responsibility for the direction of our lives. Taking full responsibility of our lives is not just about paying bills or showing up for work on time. It is far more than that. We must be mindful that we have a work life, family life, social life, personal life, mental life, physical life, emotional life, and spiritual life. When we take full responsibility, it requires a lot of work on all parts of the same life. Whenever any one part is out of order, it tends to disturb all the other parts. The thing to remember is that we are a unit and the components must work together in order for the whole to operate smoothly.

I was a person who needed love. But at the same time I rejected it because it felt uncomfortable. I believe the reason was that I was taught *emotional* love not *spiritual* love. *Emotional* love is driven by feelings or emotions and there are always strings attached – sometimes those strings feel like chains. Emotional love is about *what have you done for me lately* and it will not stand the test of time. It's like a light switch that can be turned off and on at will. Emotional love is the kind of love that makes a person hide in the bushes or throw bricks through car window. The kind of love that makes us *not want the person but don't want* to see that individual with anybody else. Emotional love borders on obsession. It would have us commit murder because "the object of our affection" left us; we don't even think that, once we kill them, that person is gone forever. A life driven by emotional love will make us do some pretty sick things.

On the other side is spiritual love. Spiritual love is coming to an understanding that we are all connected to each other at the level of spirit. It is realizing that there is *no big you* or *little me* – it is just us. Spiritual love understands that when you hurt, we hurt; when you laugh, we laugh. Not only are we connected to each other, we are also connected to our environment, and when we destroy it, we actually destroy ourselves.

I can ride through any neighborhood in the middle of the night, look at the environment, and gauge how people in that area feel about themselves. Our outside environment is merely a reflection of our inside environment. Keep in mind that everything responds to love, even the things we think are not alive. For example, if you don't love and take care of your car, watch how neglect will destroy it. This holds true for everything. *Spiritual Love is a law.* Let us continue to work to enforce this law.

The Law of Attraction

If we want to mentally free ourselves from the prison of negative thoughts, the law of attraction is vital to understand. This law states that we attract the thoughts that conform to what we believe in our hearts. Thoughts are simply the spiritual connection between what we believe and what God creates. It is how our beliefs become physical things. It doesn't matter what we say, it is what we believe that will determine the thoughts we attract. It is important to understand this because thoughts are living things that have the energy connected to them of whatever the thoughts were about. For example, when the thought of smoking crack cocaine comes into my head, the energy of that thought makes my stomach turn and I get nervous. This is when we get the illusion of demons attacking us. In actuality, it is the energy connected to the thoughts that causes the pain. When our lives have been full of hurt and pain, we tend to attract negative thoughts. Remember, the law states that we attract those thoughts that conform to what we believe. Because we were never taught how to use our minds correctly, we break this law unknowingly and pay for it with our lives. It all goes back to the beginning of our lives where we formed our beliefs and began to attract the thoughts of those beliefs. Many of the people around me thrived on, and lived in, negativity so my belief system was formed in negativity. Most of the thoughts I attracted were negative; when they were positive I paid them no mind.

Here's an example of how attraction works in the mind and shows up as a thing in the world. Say someone gets out of an abusive relationship and a few months later they seem to get into another abusive relationship. This happens because deep down at the core of their being, there is the belief that relationships are hurtful. Subconsciously, they believe relationships are bad but consciously try to get into another relationship by being on guard for the bad people. Without understanding the law that we get out of life what we believe and not what we want, that abused person constantly attracts abusers because it is what they believe; not necessarily what they want. As a result of believing that relationships are hurtful, they get into one bad relationship after another. Then, they decide to just stay out of relationships for a while and believe that taking a "break" is going to solve their problem. We cannot stop our beliefs and thoughts from becoming our reality in our physical world; so, if we cannot stop them, we must learn to change them. To change the results, we must change the beliefs, which will, in turn, attract different thoughts and manifest better things in our physical world.

This operation of the law of attraction is true in all areas of our lives and cannot be amended or changed. If I keep failing at everything I start, I need to look at what I believe about success and failure. I believed that having dreams come true and being successful were for other people, not for me. Because I believed that, I always attracted thoughts of failure, limitation, and lack. People go into business with the belief that it might not work; so they attract the thoughts and situations to themselves that cause the business to fail. When we start any project with negative beliefs, we have already set failure in motion so the results are what they are supposed to be. When we expect failure, it will come. Before we start anything, let's look *honestly* at ourselves and work on the beliefs that may defeat us. The work it will take to change our belief system is hard, long, and continuous. We must feed our minds until our minds start to feed us the stuff we fed it. When the thoughts come that may defeat us, let them through but keep focusing on what we're working to accomplish. This is why we must go back in our lives and forgive those who wronged us so that we can let go of the pain. Holding onto the pain only attracts thoughts of pain. Our mind is spiritual and is the place where attraction happens. We must be conscious of what we focus on because tomorrow it may cost us our lives.

As of the writing of this book, I've been on the speaking circuit for approximately five years. I haven't made any real money yet; however, because I believe this is my purpose, I attract the thoughts that are making it happen. I don't focus on *how long* I've been doing it because it might make me frustrated and I might revert back to negative thinking. Time only pertains to the physical world; the spirit doesn't use a clock or calendar. It's hard to stay up mentally all the time so some "down time" is healthy, but don't stay down too long. It's critical to make or buy audiotapes of powerful positive information and listen to them at least five times a week. By doing this, even if your conscious mind drifts, your subconscious mind is still recording. Winning and losing is a direct result of what we believe. Everything is a product of our beliefs and is manifested through our thoughts.

Intuition

Intuition is a universal law that tells us what to do and where to go. *Intuition is God talking to us.* Only God can know something before it's known in the physical world. We are not capable of seeing the whole picture so intuition is a preview. It's a knowing before we go; it's living the journey in our minds before we start the trip.

Intuition is a direct line from God to us through our minds. To the world, it may seem like we are lost or misdirected but the world doesn't know what we know. The truths that are spoken in me are for me, because the truth about my life has only been given to me – only I can hear it. The truth about your life has only been given to you and only you can hear it. This is what following your heart means. It's that still, sure voice from within that says to start something, it doesn't matter what. It could be to start your own business, write a book, or become an actor/actress – only you know.

The problems come when we ask others what they think we should do and they can only give us their opinion. Usually we ask people who have never done anything with their own lives, besides play it safe, and suggest that is what we should do with ours. That's like asking a bricklayer to do electrical work. Not to trust ourselves is breaking the law of intuition and the punishment will be a boring and routine driven life. Intuition without action will begin to eat at us like a cancer. If our lives are driven by emotions, intuition will have to take a backseat because emotions are very powerful when they are in charge. These are just some of the main spiritual laws of life that must be understood and adhered to in order to live the life we were all born to live.

Attunement

Attunement is making the connection between the mind and the spirit of God within us so that we might stop searching and become guided through life. Do not confuse attunement with atonement. Atonement is about making something right while attunement is about connecting to the spirit to live right.

Attunement means "to bring into accord, to become as one, to walk in harmony with self." Harmony means, "too bring into agreement, to combine all that is different into a beautiful whole." If we are to be successful as human beings, we must attune or bring together the body and spirit, through the mind, as one. I use the word human being just to make a statement because what we are is indescribable. We are energy and information, having a time and location event called life that will last for years. Our spirit is the energy that operates off of the information, surrounded by a body that allows us to be located in life for an amount of time. Attunement is about mentally connecting to that part of us that is unchangeable and indescribable – our spirit. When our minds are connected to the part of us that is changeable – our ego – we become led by emotions. When our minds are connected to our ego, which is memory of past physical experience, it makes us outward people. To be outward means that we dress up instead of growing up; that we criticize instead of looking at ourselves.

Outward people are sacred of everything. They don't take risks and they play it safe all their lives. In the end, outward people have done very little to bring Heaven to earth. Outward people always need the approval and acceptance of others to feel good about themselves. When they complete something, they need to ask at least 10 people whether or not they did a good job, even if it was their best. They have a hard time patting themselves on the back and saying job well done, so their whole life is just an illusion. It's an illusion because they're living through the opinions of others, instead of thinking and doing for themselves. This is *your life* and only you can live it or give away your power by trying to please or worry about what others might say or do.

How is an outward person created? When we are born, our parents and the people around us begin to force their beliefs and concepts of life down our throats. Many of the beliefs and concepts shoved down our throats as a child pertained to the physical world, not the spiritual. The physical world became our only point of reference so we became physically oriented. To be physically oriented makes us outward people because we get all of our decision-making information from the outside world. We ignore internal signs that tell us what to do and what not to do, so our lives are run by circumstances. The process of becoming an outward person starts early in life under the guise of "raising them right." Our parents begin the *don't do this or don't do that* cycle until we become *conditioned to respond* to life and not take an active role in it. The world is full of responders, those people who respond to, and not act on what they know to be true in their minds and souls for themselves. Outward people burn a lot of energy denying the truths that ring loud and clear in their minds. The spirit is always telling us what to do at all times but, because we have a choice, we can ignore that inner voice and suffer. To be out of attunement with the inner-spirit keeps us from living the life we were meant to live.

Now, let's talk about the other side of the coin – the inward person. When the mind is connected to the unchangeable part – our spirit, we become inward driven people. This means that we would like for other people to like us but if they don't, so be it. It won't stop us from going forward in life. We approve and accept ourselves. Inward people have a knowing about where they are going and refuse to be sidetracked by other people's opinions. We take risks in an effort to experience more of life instead of playing it safe until life becomes stale. Decision-making is our best asset and taking the heat for those decisions is our source of strength. There is an internal boldness about an inward driven person that can be seen sometimes as arrogance.

How do we become inward driven people after our entire upbringing is outward oriented? The first thing is to be willing to take risks and do something bigger than where we are in life at this moment. That may mean getting out of a dead relationship or finding a new job, or setting some

217

folks straight. Acquiring new information to change our beliefs and conceptions of life is a must, and acting on that new information is vital to change. Inward driven people have a willingness to stand alone for what we know to be true to us, regardless of what others might say. When we look at all the people we call great, notice that they stood and took the heat for what they believed. It is only through unshakable faith in what we believe can an inward driven person become great.

Your greatness is calling…will you answer the call?

CONCLUSION

I've talked about a lot of different things pertaining to living because life is not a one-course subject. We must major in a lot of minors. There is so much we must know in order to be functional that too many of us are ignorant of.

Every human being is a center of creation. We are always creating as a result of our choices...whether it is right or wrong, positive or negative. Not to understand this fact has led a great many of us into despair where we feel that we need someone to save us. There is no one before us or who will come after us who can save us from our choices. We must learn to save ourselves by choice.

This book is dedicated to the people who are willing to look honestly into the mirror at themselves, and call things the way they are...*not the way we pretend them to be.* Emotional Prisoner is a word picture of a spiritual life served behind mental bars where the jailer is our emotions. Once the spirit becomes locked-up in the mind, our lives become driven by routine and appearance. The only thing that frees the spirit is a willingness to be honest about our entire life, not just what I call "acceptable truth." Acceptable truth is where we say the easy stuff to save face but end up losing our behinds.

Here's a word of encouragement: There is no one who is totally healed. Everybody, at some level, is mentally sick. It is important to understand that our lives will not get better without our help. Mental illness does not get better on its own. There must be a willingness to expose the hurt to the light of truth. Truth heals; lies keep the mind sick.

When the mind is run by emotions, we end up serving time instead of time serving us. We don't have to go to jail to be locked up; far too many of us are incarcerated in life. In order to parole our spirits from serving time because it's our spirits that are locked behind negative thoughts, we must work on changing the only part of our mind that can be changed. That is our belief system.

Beliefs are the cornerstone of our lives – the first brick in the wall or the first nail in the new house. *Everything starts and ends with belief.*

To have a great physical existence, we must start by building a solid foundation of new beliefs to erect our lives upon. I use the word "build" because it means, "to construct or create." Our *old* belief system must be torn down and rebuilt with *new* information. Remember that our belief system is simply information we have picked up from the physical world and have internalized as truth – even if it is not. All of our beliefs are stored in our minds controlled by our egos. Our spiritual heart is where everything springs forth.

Every one of us can use *a heart transplant* – not the *tangible* one that is in our chest pumping blood but the *intangible* one that is in our minds that pumps information.

Make the commitment to yourself to change your life, no matter the emotional cost. The cost of staying the same is much higher.

In closing always remember *winners do what they have to do; losers do what they want to do.*

God bless, and have a great life.

ABOUT THE AUTHOR

JOSÉ VILLEGAS III was born and raised in New Orleans, Louisiana. He is the middle child of three, and comes from humble beginnings. José struggled mentally and emotionally as young boy and decided to drop out of school in the 8th grade. At age 17, he joined the United States Army just to escape his environment.

Because José had no understanding of himself, he ended up hopeless, homeless, and addicted to crack cocaine.

As of the writing of this book, José has turned his life completely around. He went back to school to better himself, embarked on a phenomenal personal development journey, and has been sober for 11 years.

Today José is a much sought-after speaker and a great writer who carries his *message of hope* to the masses in an effort to encourage others to begin to examine themselves and *choose to change* for the better.